Shane does a terrific job tying the practicality of managing money to God's Word and to our Lord and Savior, Jesus. I recommend this book heartily.

RON BLUE, founder of Kingdom Advisors; bestselling author of *Master Your Money*

Whole Heart Finances is a must-read for anyone seeking to align their financial journey with their faith. Embrace the wisdom within these pages, and embark on a journey toward lasting financial well-being, guided by faith and purpose.

MARCY PALOS, president and CEO of RestoreLA-CDC

Dr. Enete's students can attest to the transforming influence of his financial-planning principles. I know this firsthand, for they have told me. Readers of his new book will benefit from the same deep well of Shane's rich insights formed over a career of investment research and his example of sacrificial stewardship.

BARRY H. COREY, president, Biola University

Whole Heart Finances should be required reading for all church leadership, followers of Jesus, pastoral studies, and small groups. It's the gold standard for synthesizing sound financial research and spirituality. Shane has the wisdom of a world-class financial advisor and the heart of a pastor. His financial wisdom is safe.

RENÉ J. MOLINA, executive pastor of RLA Church and PhD candidate

Dr. Enete gently invites us to think deeply, theologically, and practically about the misunderstood topic of finances and the heart. His approach is welcoming and real, encouraging us with the truth that Jesus surprises us with delightful things when we give our hearts and finances to him. A must-read for any classroom or church finance course.

OSCAR MERLO, PhD; director, Center for the Study of the Work and Ministry of the Holy Spirit Today

Clear. Succinct. Wise. Christ-focused. Dr. Enete has combined biblical wisdom with financial savvy to help Christians know how to properly orient toward finances, investments, and generous sharing. I am happy to recommend it.

KENNETH BERDING, PhD, author of *Paul's Thorn in the Flesh* and *Walking in the Spirit*

Shane Enete's book gets to the heart of the matter! Christians can't serve God *and* money, so Shane teaches them how to joyfully serve God *with* money. I highly recommend that Christians everywhere put into practice what Shane's book teaches.

BRIAN KLUTH, author of the bestselling *40 Day Generous*

With a mix of personal testimony, wit, and truth from Scripture, Shane turns this "dangerous" topic of money into an invitation to experience more intimacy with Jesus in every area of your life.

NICK BREACH, vice president, Compass—Finances God's Way

Whole Heart Finances has a solid biblical foundation for managing finances with Jesus at the center. It is the first book I would recommend for Christians who want a biblical perspective and real-life wisdom on stewarding finances.

ADAM W. DAY, associate professor of New Testament language and literature, Tyndale Theological Seminary, The Netherlands

Whole Heart Finances is just what the subtitle describes: *A Jesus-Centered Guide to Managing Your Money with Joy.* Recognizing the biblical idea that one's "heart" is not merely the seat of emotions but also the center of the will, Enete challenges readers to "bring your whole heart," "spend with your whole heart," "guard your whole heart," and "save with your whole heart." If you are a follower of Jesus and read only one book on managing your personal finances, this should be it.

DOUGLAS S. HUFFMAN, professor of New Testament and dean of academic programs, Talbot School of Theology at Biola University

Whole Heart Finances provides a wonderful combination of compelling stories that illustrate biblical financial wisdom and practical ways to implement these lessons right away. This book will challenge you to consider new perspectives on wealth accumulation, debt, giving, retirement, and so much more.

CODY HOBELMANN, CFP®, cohost of *The Finish Line Podcast*

Shane Enete's insights into stewardship centered on Jesus are profound. In fact, I read part 1 twice before moving on to the rest of the book. I love the way he sets the foundation and builds on it. I kept thinking that all seven of my kids (ages 19 to 31) should read *Whole Heart Finances*. I "wholeheartedly" recommend this book.

DAVID H. WILLS, president emeritus, National Christian Foundation

Dr. Shane Enete is among the most thoughtful leaders on biblical stewardship to emerge in my generation. I admire his work for its depth of theology, practical application, and academically informed rigor. I loved *Whole Heart Finances* and strongly recommend it for every Christ-follower!

JOHN CORTINES, coauthor of *God and Money* and *True Riches*

WH❤LE
HEART
FINANCES

A Jesus-Centered Guide to
Managing Your Money with Joy

SHANE ENETE,
PhD, CFA, CFP®

AspirePress

Whole Heart Finances:
A Jesus-Centered Guide to Managing Your Money with Joy
Copyright © 2024 by Delightful Dollar, Inc.
Published by Aspire Press
An imprint of Tyndale House Ministries
Carol Stream, Illinois
www.hendricksonrose.com

ISBN: 978-1-4964-8328-7

The views and opinions expressed in this book are those of the author(s) and do not necessarily express the views of Tyndale House Ministries or Aspire Press. The information in this resource is intended as a guideline only. Please consult qualified financial professionals regarding individual concerns.

Tyndale House Ministries and Aspire Press are in no way liable for any content, change of content, or activity for the works listed. Citation of a work does not mean endorsement of all its contents or of other works by the same author.

All author royalties are donated to a charity that advances Christ-centered financial education.

"A Liturgy for the Paying of the Bills" is taken from *Every Moment Holy* (Rabbit Room Press), by Douglas Kaine McKelvey. Used with permission.

All Scripture emphasis has been added by the author.

All Scripture quotations, unless otherwise indicated, are taken from the Holy Bible, New International Version,® NIV.® Copyright ©1973, 1978, 1984, 2011 by Biblica, Inc.® Used by permission of Zondervan. All rights reserved worldwide. www.zondervan.com. The "NIV" and "New International Version" are trademarks registered in the United States Patent and Trademark Office by Biblica, Inc.®

Scripture quotations marked ESV are from The ESV® Bible (The Holy Bible, English Standard Version®), copyright © 2001 by Crossway, a publishing ministry of Good News Publishers. Used by permission. All rights reserved.

Scripture quotation marked NASB is taken from the (NASB®) New American Standard Bible,® copyright © 1960, 1971, 1977, 1995, 2020 by The Lockman Foundation. Used by permission. All rights reserved. www.lockman.org. Scripture quotation marked NASB 1995 is taken from the 1995 edition.

Scripture quotation marked NCV is taken from the New Century Version.® Copyright © 2005 by Thomas Nelson, Inc. Used by permission. All rights reserved.

Scripture quotation marked NKJV is taken from the New King James Version,® copyright © 1982 by Thomas Nelson. Used by permission. All rights reserved.

Scripture quotations marked NLT are taken from the *Holy Bible*, New Living Translation, copyright ©1996, 2004, 2015 by Tyndale House Foundation. Used by permission of Tyndale House Publishers, Carol Stream, Illinois 60188. All rights reserved.

Photos under license from Shutterstock.com.

Printed in the United States of America
011023VP

CONTENTS

INTRODUCTION

What dominated [Jesus's] mind was not
the living but the giving of his life.
JOHN STOTT, *THE CROSS OF CHRIST*

I love and hate the game of Monopoly. I love it because it involves money, and that is what I teach about for a living. I hate it because it is tiresome, stressful, and often never ends.

But there is one game of Monopoly that I will never forget. Many years ago, when I was with a group of friends for game night, everyone groaned when our host brought it out. We eventually relented and started to play, but as my friends began to make more money than I did, feelings of resentment and envy crept into my heart. My eyes darkened with every roll of the dice, hoping to get ahead.

This burdensome spirit began to overtake everyone playing, and soon I noticed something peculiar out of the corner of my eye—a hand quickly pulling away from the center pile of cash. A few turns later, I noticed it again. In that moment, I was certain I had found a cheater! The third time it happened, I pointed my finger and yelled, "Cheater! Give us back our pooled parking money!"

After I accused my friend, he blushed and said, "I wasn't cheating ... I was giving." A long pause in the room was quickly followed by barrels of laughter. My friend had just admitted that he was secretly giving back some of his Monopoly money as a tithe! It was such a surprising and delightful behavior that we all wanted in.

As the game progressed, everyone started to get creative with how they would secretly give back to the parking pile, including sly behind-the-back moves. My friend's generosity had completely transformed the game. We were still trying to play by the rules, and we were still competing to win, but a new element had been added that made it a joy to play.

Like the game Monopoly, making money decisions every day is a strategic game that we both love and hate (perhaps we mostly hate it). It is a game that is tiresome and stressful and truly doesn't end. Study after study confirms that Americans consider money their top source of anxiety.[1]

But it doesn't have to be this way. There is an element we can introduce that will completely transform our experience. It will turn the game of managing our finances from one of fear and dread to one of trust and joy. If you were to say that this element is generosity, you would be only partially correct.

In his book *Give and Take*, Wharton professor Adam Grant lays out a brilliant case for how generosity benefits a person's life. In one example, researchers map the energy of people the same way a galaxy would be mapped. Those who act as *givers* are compared to suns in our galaxy, casting light that makes everyone around them bigger. Those who act as *takers* are mapped as black holes, sucking energy from those around them and making everyone smaller.[2] The conclusion of the book is that we should all become givers in order to reap the great benefits of generosity.

> **Making money decisions every day is a strategic game that is tiresome and stressful. *But it doesn't have to be this way.***

While this conclusion is valid and would certainly improve our finances, I propose that it is both too hard and not ambitious enough. It is too hard because we often think too much about ourselves and not enough about others. Personally, I was not born a very generous person, so I worry about whether I can simply "become a giver" by my own effort.

Becoming a giver is also not ambitious enough. Instead of settling for the light that we could shine by ourselves, why not draw near to *the* Light of the world, the Sun of suns, the ultimate Giver? Jesus Christ is all of these things, and his light of generosity is so bright that everyone around him shines and shimmers simply because they are near to him.

The primary element to add to managing our finances, then, is Jesus Christ. You may object to this idea, thinking, *Jesus doesn't really approve of money. Like he said to the rich young man who asked how he could gain eternal life, Jesus is just going to tell me to sell everything I own.*[3] Variations of this thought have led many Christians to separate Jesus from their finances. While this may feel safer, it can never be a reality if you are a follower of Jesus, because the truth is that "Christ lives within you" (Romans 8:10 NLT). Through the Holy Spirit, Christ inhabits your heart.

If you choose to believe that Jesus is separate from your finances, you are not only darkening your world as you draw away from the Light of the world; you are also fracturing your heart. You're like a newly married person who wants to know everything about your spouse, but the moment they mention anything related to their finances, you plug your ears and shout, "Keep that to yourself! That is none of my business." Can you imagine the stress of a marriage that is fractured in this way?

We do the same thing when we say to Jesus, *You are in charge of my spiritual life, but let's keep separate accounts when it comes to my finances.* Going out alone with your finances ensures that you will have a fractured heart since Jesus already lives in your heart. You are acting in a way that is not consistent with your true self.

A whole heart is one that fully embraces Jesus with every decision that your heart truly cares about, particularly regarding money. If involving Jesus in your money decisions seems odd, this is likely because you have only really thought of him as spiritual. Yet Jesus is very much physical! In Scripture, he eats, drinks, and has a physical body—one that he inhabits even to this day! Jesus said in the Gospel of Luke, "Touch me and see; a ghost does not have flesh and bones, as you see I have…. Do you have anything here to eat?" (Luke 24:39–41).

Jesus completely understands your material needs, and he completely understands that they require you to spend money. He likes good food and even pretty things—including Carolina barbeque, Guatemalan coffee, and Swedish furniture—and he is "all in" as we enjoy them. Once this reality is woven into your daily financial life, you will find that every dollar becomes a joy to manage.

As you may already know, Jesus Christ is the most joyful person you will ever meet, so if you invite him into the daily game of managing your finances, you will find joy. And just like my friend in my Monopoly story, Jesus will do surprising and delightful things, leaving you with an open invitation to imitate his creative play with your money. Managing your money will become a wide highway for you to love him and others in a deeper way.

Whole Heart Finances will draw out what it looks like to fully incorporate the reality of your union with Christ into your daily finances. Each chapter will begin by gazing upon the person of Jesus Christ, who is a blazing light of generosity, and then it will highlight specific actions that can help you respond to the light you are seeing.

If you invite Jesus into the daily game of managing your finances, he will do surprising and delightful things.

Part 1 (chapters 1–3) will introduce how to *bring your whole heart to Jesus* as you relate to your finances. Then you will be united with him in a fun and joyful way as you make spending, saving, and giving decisions.

Part 2 (chapters 4–7) will discuss the importance of *looking, tracking, and spending plans* so that you can *apply and express your whole heart* as you spend money.

Part 3 (chapters 8–10) will discuss how to responsibly relate to *credit and debt* so that you can *guard your whole heart* as you relate to your finances.

Part 4 (chapters 11–15) will discuss how you can use the tools of *saving and investing* to become more intentional in your *response to Jesus's great generosity* toward you. Chapter 15 will bring all the financial elements together so you can dream big about how Jesus can use *your own financial plan* to help redeem and restore our broken world.

Let us begin!

Please note that an appendix filled with helpful tools and resources is available at wholeheartfinances.com. There you can also find a four-lesson small group study designed to teach key concepts from this book in a highly visual way.

PART 1

BRING YOUR WHOLE HEART

Invite Jesus into Your Financial Life

I have been crucified with Christ and I no
longer live, but Christ lives in me.

GALATIANS 2:20

CHAPTER 1

THE MOST DANGEROUS QUESTION

Whatever you do, work at it with all your heart.

COLOSSIANS 3:23

I like money. It's not that I want to be rich; there is just something exciting about seeing the face of George Washington on a crisp dollar bill. Often when I get lost in bank statements and bills, however, I may let out a long sigh or squint my eyes and furrow my brow. My seven-year-old daughter, Sage, does this too whenever she thinks about money. She is her father's daughter.

One evening at bedtime I was telling Sage and my six-year-old son, Silas, a story about a train that was leading them through a forest. Their destination was a large mansion, with many exciting and magical rooms. I ended by explaining that this was a picture of what the kingdom of heaven will be like. My children were not prepared for this plot twist and immediately jumped out of their beds in excitement, exclaiming, "We can't believe you told us a story that is actually *real*, Daddy!"

For the next thirty minutes, we talked about the joy of life with Jesus in heaven while Sage and Silas danced around their beds. Eventually my wife, Tammy, and I said goodnight and left the room. Later Tammy and I were in the middle of a conversation when we heard little footsteps in the hallway. Turning, we saw Sage quietly placing something on the carpet. She beamed and giggled as she said, "This is for Jesus." Then she ran back to her room as quickly as she had appeared.

As Tammy and I set our eyes on the clear bag of coins and bills, we started to cry when we realized it was Sage's entire life savings! She had spent a whole year building it up—a long time for a seven-year-old. I had not brought up the subject of giving with her that night, and yet here was her natural response to the gospel of Jesus Christ. In that moment, my daughter, in her unicorn pajamas, did not have a furrowed brow, and she did not let out a long sigh. Instead, she skipped and giggled all the way back to her bedroom.

Am I Supposed to Give It All Away?

After our tears subsided, Tammy and I continued our earlier conversation. But I was a bit distracted. Sage's actions had prompted a very dangerous, haunting question to brood in the back of my head; probably *the* most dangerous question a Christian can ask, in fact: *Is that what I'm supposed to do—give away all of my money?*

As I dared to ask this question, suddenly my daughter's joyful act was not so cute. Instead, it was threatening. Like Cain, who was jealous of his brother's generosity (Genesis 4:5), my face became downcast. A defensive spirit rose up in my heart, and thoughts of justification filled my mind: *Sage wouldn't be able to eat if I gave away my life savings. According to 1 Timothy 5:8, I would be worse than an unbeliever if I didn't provide for my relatives. It's a scriptural truth, so I don't have to think about this anymore.*

I am not the only one to contemplate this weighty matter. There is a hidden assumption among many Christians that Jesus is eager to surprise us with this dangerous question. When I survey adults about what they think Jesus would say if they honestly asked him what to do with their money, just about everyone assumes he would tell them to sell everything and follow him.

A comedy sketch by the popular duo Key & Peele highlights the fear of this dangerous question among the American Christian church. In this short video, a home fellowship group is fervently praying for God to show them his will for them. A bright light shines onto the living room coffee table, and God begins to speak. The group eagerly listens as God lovingly instructs them to sell everything they own and start serving the poor. At this point, everyone is uncomfortably silent, clearly unable to accept God's proposition.

Finally someone yells, "This house is haunted!" Chaos ensues as everyone screams and runs out the door.[4]

The Haunting of a Teenager

This was also not the first time I had been haunted by this dangerous question. In fact, it is a question that, in many ways, has defined my working life. At the age of fifteen, my uncle handed me a book—*How to Invest $50–$5,000*. It was the title that hooked me. Fifty dollars was an achievable number to me, so investing suddenly became a real possibility. I immediately went to the library and checked out all the books I could find on the topic of investing. I just had to learn more. I didn't particularly desire to have wealth, but I was captivated by the idea of managing it.

My passion for managing money, however, would soon collide with my budding relationship with Jesus. Two years earlier, I nearly died when I fell two stories off a balcony and landed on an iron-rod fence. While recovering in the hospital, I was powerfully changed as I sensed Jesus's constant abiding presence on the right side of the room. It was a taste of heaven that still lingers in my heart today. His presence communicated an unreserved, warm, and wild love for me—by the Creator of the universe, no less! It was just too wonderful.

> There is a hidden assumption among many Christians that Jesus is eager to surprise us with "the most dangerous question."

Even though I was a helpless bag of bones in that hospital bed, I felt known and cherished, and that made me want to follow Jesus with *all* of myself. But as a fifteen-year-old teenager, "myself" now included a love for managing money. As I grew more and more involved in the world of profit and wealth, it felt like I was growing further away from Jesus, my first love, who cherishes sacrifice and dependence. That's when I first started to wonder, *Am I supposed to give away all of my money?*

In high school, I sought more industry and educational knowledge to help me answer this most dangerous question. I would often peruse the Money and Economics section in my local bookstore, vowing that I would read every book in that aisle. During my twenties and thirties, true to my vow, I earned multiple certifications (CFA, CFP,® CAIA), a master's in mathematical finance, and a PhD in personal financial planning. I also worked at large money-management firms for over a decade, helping shepherd billions of dollars in the investment markets.

Yet throughout all of this, it seems I heard only one answer to the most dangerous question: "You are a fool to even ask it!" For example, one day my boss and I began to talk about the purpose of wealth. I gently introduced the idea that complete financial independence entails a significant loss where you will likely shut yourself off from relying on God, who has unlimited resources. I still remember the incredulous look on his face that said, *What is this guy doing in this business? What a nut!*

My Unbaptized Paycheck

During this time, I hated being so conflicted about Jesus and money. I especially didn't like thinking about the most dangerous question. *Perhaps I should just stop asking it,* I thought. Because I could not reconcile a life with Jesus with a life of managing money, I came up with a solution: I should separate my financial life from my relationship with Jesus. *Yes!*

I am not the first person to think of separating part of my life from Jesus. During Charlemagne's conquering days, a group of soldiers heard his edict that they must get baptized. Feeling the urgency to do so before they conquered a nearby village, the soldiers found a local priest and a river. Then something peculiar happened: They raised their swords high in the air so their hands would not get wet. To their credit, these soldiers understood what baptism meant. They left their sword-wielding hands unbaptized since they did not know how to reconcile their engagement in war with a life surrendered to Jesus Christ.[5]

I performed a very similar act, except it was my paycheck that I excluded from the holy waters of baptism. The moment I decided that I could not accept Jesus's dangerous question (which I assumed he was going to ask me), I left my paychecks dry and unbaptized. At the time, I thought it was a brilliant idea. As I "submerged in the water," it's likely that I subconsciously repeated the following words: *Because you, Jesus, are probably unreasonable with your demands about money, I choose to bear full financial responsibility in my life and give you every other part of me.*

I did this because I was confused about how a life surrendered to Jesus could be reconciled with the financial responsibilities of saving money, paying bills, and eating out. But I was still a passionate Christian since this act of mine was not a complete rejection. After all, Jesus was able to have every part of me except that paycheck. What I did could be likened to marrying my wife, then on our honeymoon, lovingly gazing into her eyes and saying, "I presume you have crazy ideas when it comes to money, so I don't want us to talk about money together. In fact, you may *never* discuss money with me. Love you! Hugs and kisses."

Financial Wreckage

One sign that you have adopted this bad solution of fleeing from Jesus with your finances is that you are anxious about money. For yet another year, Americans have listed money as their number one source of anxiety.[6] Consider these lines from the poem "Worry about Money," published by Kathleen Raine in 1949:

> *Wearing worry about money like a hair shirt*
> *I lie down in my bed and wrestle with my angel.*[7]

"Wearing worry about money" may sum up how you feel at the moment. Dr. Galen Buckwalter, who studies financial trauma, found that more than 20% of Americans are suffering from financial stress that meets the clinical definition of post-traumatic stress disorder (PTSD).[8]

Additionally, research conducted for my PhD dissertation showed that having negative emotions in general was associated with lower income, lower net worth, and lower financial satisfaction. These negative emotions fostered an inability to look past one's immediate needs in order to plan for a better future.[9]

We see poor financial behavior everywhere. In fact, roughly 60% of Americans would not be able to pay for a $1,000 emergency with savings.[10] The average American has over $5,000 of credit card debt and $39,000 of student-loan debt.[11] This debt has also dramatically heightened stress among Americans and lowered their overall health and well-being.[12]

An Incomplete Remedy

Given these financial problems, would everything be made right if people cobbled together higher savings and ruthlessly eliminated their debts? And since it has also been shown that only 35% of Americans are financially literate, will all be made well if we pair higher financial literacy with higher savings and no debt?[13]

While achieving higher financial savings does help soothe our worry (and this book will also help you in that way), it is not a complete remedy. Consider that our society has never been richer and yet has never been more worried about money.[14] Many times, becoming more stable with money simply moves us from worrying about money while lying on a straw bed to worrying about money while lounging on a California king–sized bed.

For example, a prominent money talk show host once received a phone call from a school bus driver who had diligently performed every good financial behavior, and now she had a net worth of a million dollars. And yet her voice quivered over the radio as she whispered, "I am terrified about not having enough."

An expansive survey of 165 super-rich households (those with over $25 million) found very disturbing results:

> The respondents turn out to be a generally dissatisfied lot, whose money has contributed to deep anxieties involving love, work, and family. Indeed, they are frequently dissatisfied even with their sizable fortunes. Most of them still do not consider themselves financially secure; for that, they say, they would require on average one-quarter more wealth than they currently possess.… One respondent, the heir to an enormous fortune, says that what matters most to him is his Christianity, and that his greatest aspiration is "to love the Lord, my family, and my friends." He also reports that he wouldn't feel financially secure until he had $1 billion in the bank.[15]

As you can see, often financial worries do not go away, even with no debt, a comfortable emergency fund, and more than $25 million.

Taming the Most Dangerous Question

Remember the story at the beginning of this chapter, where Sage's radical generosity caused me to ask the most dangerous question again—*Am I supposed to give all of my money away?* She, like her name suggests, was also the one who guided me toward the wisdom I needed to answer it.

One lazy Sunday afternoon, we were watching an episode from the hit series *The Chosen.* After Jesus healed Peter's mother-in-law, she sprang out of bed and started to prepare refreshments for everyone, yelling out, "Does Jesus like goat cheese?" Jesus replied, "Yes, I love goat cheese."

At that moment, Sage's eyes lit up, and she immediately ran over to me, declaring in joy, "I love goat cheese too!" Tammy and I both teared

Our society has never been richer and yet has never been more worried about money.

up at such a beautiful picture of our child enjoying Jesus and her heavenly Father. After we settled down again, I suddenly realized that Sage, through her thrill in sharing a love of goat cheese with Jesus, had actually solved the mystery around the most dangerous question! Her declaration elegantly captured an incredible chain of events:

1. Jesus took on flesh.

2. He developed all sorts of interesting personal tastes, including a love of goat cheese (maybe).

3. He died on the cross to take the punishment for our sins.

4. He gave his followers the Holy Spirit through his work on the cross.

5. Jesus ascended to heaven with a physical body and (maybe) still loves goat cheese.

The end result of this sequence is that Jesus very much cares about our physical bodies, too, which require finances so we can be fed, clothed, sheltered, and looked after. He cares at a much deeper level than we can imagine because we have been mysteriously united to him through the work of the Holy Spirit: "I have been crucified with Christ and I no longer live, but Christ lives in me" (Galatians 2:20). Our body is now a part of his body (1 Corinthians 6:15).

Jesus Christ gave this incredible gift of himself to us while we were still separated from him because of our sin. If we accept his gift, we become dead to sin and dead to any money laws that may try to condemn us. *We are people of grace now*, so there are no more dangerous questions. There is no longer any need to worry that Jesus will reject us if we do not give away all of our money. Whether we do or do not, the grace of Jesus ensures that we will remain his treasure no matter what.

Grace and Whole Heart Finances

One beautiful sunny day, a student walked into my office with a question related to his stock portfolio. Before offering my thoughts, I asked, "Have you sought counsel from Jesus?" He was caught completely off guard. Although he didn't say it, his perplexed look communicated the same sentiment I have seen expressed on so many other faces: *What does* he *have to do with it?*

Unfortunately, when we separate Jesus from our finances, we are simply fracturing our hearts. Put another way, we are not managing money with our *whole heart*, and that makes us feel anxious, alienated, and alone with our money. The moment we make financial decisions without Jesus, where our paychecks remain dry and unbaptized, our "wearing worry about money" will likely remain.

> The grace of Jesus ensures that we will remain his treasure no matter what.

As Christians, we are not like the rich young man who had to decide between Jesus and his money. Every Christian who has accepted Jesus as their Lord and Savior is now mysteriously united to him, so it is a false choice to either include Jesus in our financial decisions or remain separated from him.

Distrusting Jesus with our finances is called *fractured heart finances*, where we end up experiencing great anxiety and alienation as we navigate our finances alone. By contrast, when we place our faith in the risen Christ, we join our whole heart with his, and a whole heart is not afraid to approach him about money. This paradoxical life is called *whole heart finances*. Because our whole heart is united to Christ through the Holy Spirit, our finances become an opportunity for deep, responsive worship.

To fully embrace the grace of Jesus will likely create fertile ground for us to respond with a radical generosity (2 Corinthians 8–9), but we are also called to be faithful in our stewardship of the money that is being entrusted to us (Luke 16:12). If we give radically, where we never have wealth, how can we grow in our stewardship skills?

This is a tension that I want this book to completely embrace. The principles presented here will help you become financially skilled with spending plans, credit, saving, and investing while seeking to respond to Jesus's incredible generosity toward you. *Whole Heart Finances* answers practical questions such as,

- How can tracking your expenses help grow your relationship with Jesus?
- What is the best way to plan for irregular expenses?
- Should you have a credit card?
- Does it matter if your credit score is low?
- Is it financially savvy to lease a car?
- How much should you contribute to your retirement savings?
- Should you invest in the stock market? If so, in what way?
- How can you use the tools of saving and investing to maximize generous giving?

The next chapter will provide a model for how to put the elements of spending, saving, and giving together using your union with Jesus Christ as its foundation. Throughout the rest of the book, this model will act as a framework for making day-to-day financial decisions with your whole heart that is united to Jesus.

WHOLE HEART EXERCISES

WHERE ARE YOU NOW?

When I think about paying bills and saving for emergencies, I ...

☐ Ignore Jesus. [Mark any statements that apply.]

- » Jesus has nothing to do with my money.

- » Jesus is probably standing over my shoulder, shaking his head in disapproval.

- » Jesus only wants me to be poor—and I'm not okay with that.

☐ Worship Jesus. [Mark any statements that apply.]

- » Jesus cherishes being an important part of my life, and I cherish sharing my whole heart with my greatest love.

- » Jesus is incredibly wise and smart with money, and his presence only helps me become a better steward of his money.

- » I am already in-Christ, so we are in this together no matter what.

Which number best reflects Jesus's involvement in your financial life?

I DON'T THINK ABOUT JESUS								I WORSHIP JESUS	
1	2	3	4	5	6	7	8	9	10

BAPTIZE YOUR NEW MONEY

When a chick hatches, it deems whatever it first sees as its parent. This is called *imprinting*. In the same way, when money first comes into your possession, it will imprint to either (1) your old self that is dead to sin but still tries to ruin everything for you, or (2) your new self in Christ.

In the first case, the money is instantly deposited into your personal vault as "my precious money," for your use alone. Giving will be very difficult, because it will be like giving away a part of yourself.

In the second scenario, the money will naturally be imprinted as "money from my precious Father." It will be placed in your heart as something that has been given to you in the context of the church community, where the Father is the head of your household. Giving is much easier since this money was never fully imprinted to your personal vault, so giving is not like losing yourself.

❑ Look ahead to the next time you will receive money from your parents, your employer, or even the government (e.g., a tax refund). Estimate the amount: $_____.

❑ Romans 5–6 says that we are dead to sin and alive in Christ. The apostle Paul talks about us *knowing* this truth, *counting* it to be true for us personally (i.e., faith), and then *presenting* this truth before the Lord and everyone around us. For the new money you identified, take a moment to baptize it into these truths.

1. **Know:** Romans 6:10–11 says, "The death [Jesus] died, he died to sin once for all; but the life he lives, he lives to God. In the same way, count yourselves dead to sin but alive to God in Christ Jesus." In essence, you and all that you possess are dead to sin and alive in Christ. What does this mean to you?

_____

_____

_____

_____

2. Count: "To count" is an accounting term that means "to take inventory." You may know that something is true, like you have $1,000 in the bank. But you count it to be true when you actually make decisions in ways where you are "counting on" that money to be there. Reflect on how you will count it true that you are "dead to sin but alive to God in Christ Jesus."

_____

_____

_____

_____

3. Present: Just like a bride and groom present themselves as newly married, write down your intentions to present yourself and this new money as dead to sin and alive in Christ.

_____

_____

_____

_____

This new money has now been imprinted to your new self and is placed in your Father's house, fully available for whatever Jesus may want you to do with it. Whether you spend it, give it away, or save it, you are under a banner of grace.

You may need to complete this imprinting exercise with every paycheck or bank deposit since your old self will never stop trying to be the first face that your new money sees.

CHAPTER 2

THE WISDOM OF THE SEA OF GALILEE

We, who have received from the river of God's delights, pass it on.

LEANNE PAYNE, *LISTENING PRAYER*

My wife and I love to hike. While we were dating, we took a day-long hike in the Pacific Northwest, the land of rain and fog. Tammy was building up how amazing the waterfall-view was going to be at the top of the trail. We hiked for hours, deep in the woods, and when we finally reached the summit, the fog was so thick that we could only see each other! We were both pretty disappointed (but still giggly since we were newly dating).

Without much faith, I told Tammy that Jesus was going to clear the fog when I blew into it. I playfully pursed my lips, blew into the air, and waited. Incredibly, within moments, all the fog had cleared! We could see a vast lake, a powerful waterfall, and the crest of a beautiful mountain. We continued to giggle as we took it all in with awe.

Here is a crazy mystery: The King of the Universe cares about every detail of our lives. From providing daily bread to blowing away the fog on a hike, his care is truly generous and too wonderful to comprehend. "God so loved the world that he gave …" (John 3:16).

I, on the other hand, am not a naturally generous person. This is a struggle I face even to this day. Just last year, my family and I were enjoying some time poolside when a friend asked to borrow some of our sunscreen. I hesitated! My heart truly did not want to share it. In that moment, I was thinking more about conserving our $12.50 sunscreen than the well-being of my friend.

Growing up, all I wanted to do was buy pets and Transformer toys, and then save to buy more lizards, hamsters, birds, and Transformer toys. As a teenager, I did not have a single moment when I thought it would be great to be generous with my Taco Bell wages. If I did give to my church, it was with a disappointed scowl, like giving to the taxman.

In college, however, I began to think about how money could draw me into a deeper relationship with Jesus. My freshman year, I began to experiment with involving the Holy Spirit in my giving. What would happen if I simply looked around for needs to meet instead of just giving an impersonal 10%?

This became so fun, and I still remember the day I realized what God had done in my heart. I'd recently graduated and was living paycheck to paycheck as a temporary employee. One day as I was going over my spending plan, I said out loud, "How much of my paycheck do I have to keep?" Prior to this, my entire life was dominated by a very different question: "How much do I have to give?" In that moment, I couldn't help but cry.

The Economy of the Trinity

This chapter is going to explore how deep we can get with Jesus in our spending, giving, and saving. Jesus is truly *with us*. But just how close is he? Is he a buddy who gives us encouragement? A moral angel on our shoulder who stops us from ordering molten lava cake for dessert? A miser who gets angry if we save money in a 401(k) instead of giving it away?

As we saw in chapter 1, our brokenness related to money is often caused by fleeing Jesus with our financial lives. Many Christians wrongly think that Jesus is "just spiritual" and money is an unclean chore they must manage alone. But money is so fundamentally tied to the deeper things of God that the apostle Paul chose to describe the most important truth in the universe using money language! To help his readers unpack the mysteries of Jesus's work on the cross, Paul used the word *oikonomia*, which the ancient Greeks used to describe how a household should manage its resources. Here is one way to paraphrase its meaning in Ephesians 1:9–10: "[God] made us know the mystery of his will … through an economy [*oikonomia*] in which, when the times were fulfilled, he would sum up everything … under one heading: Christ!"[16]

Oikonomia comes from two Greek words: *oikos*, meaning "house," and *nemō*, meaning "tend." The latter word is related to the word *nomos*, meaning "law." The ancient Greek philosophers understood this word to mean the law that provides for the orderly management of a household.[17] Jesus used it three times in his parable of the dishonest steward (Luke 16:1–13), where the master asks his steward to give an account of his "management" (i.e., *oikonomia*) of his household. This word is often translated into English as "economy," and individuals or groups *economize* when they seek to properly manage the resources of their households.

But Paul used the word *oikonomia* in a completely new way. According to him, God managed (i.e., *oikonomia*) or *economized* his Son and Spirit in order to save us. He did this by (1) generously sending his Son, Jesus Christ, allowing him to take on flesh and the penalty for our sins by dying on the cross, and (2) sending his Holy Spirit, allowing him to indwell those who are made righteous when they accept Christ's forgiveness.

How strange of Paul to argue that Jesus Christ is a type of financial resource managed by God the Father! It seems like money and Jesus should not really intersect. Does speaking about the deep things of God as an "economy of salvation" seem in poor taste?

The answer is emphatically no, especially given that money and possessions are the second-most discussed topic in the Bible and are included in 2,350 verses.[18] If so much of the Bible discusses God and money together, then that is exactly what we should do as well.

Ephesians 1:9–10 is not the only passage in the Bible that uses a money term to describe an important spiritual topic. Consider the following as well:

- **Atonement:** "[God] forgave us all our sins, having canceled the charge of our legal indebtedness, which stood against us and condemned us; he has taken it away, nailing it to the cross" (Colossians 2:13–14). Christ's atonement for our sins is described as a financial *debt* being paid off.

- **Faith:** "Count yourselves dead to sin but alive to God in Christ Jesus" (Romans 6:11). Our act of faith in the power of the cross is described as a business owner who *counts* their inventory.

If Paul uses financial language to discuss the holy Trinity and matters of salvation, then I think it is appropriate for us to use spiritual language to gain a deeper understanding of how we should manage our money lives.

Three Keys to Christian Stewardship

Augustine once proclaimed that through the Holy Spirit, the essence of the Triune God resides *in a person*.[19] This reality needs to become the cornerstone of a Christian's personal financial planning model. Let's unpack three key ways that having the Trinity alive and active in a Christian's life will change their view of money.

Key 1: A New Heart

Before encountering the gospel, we are stuck in an "unlimited wants, limited means" world. Everything depends on us, and we must earn an income to survive. Our hearts yearn to earn! But when the Trinity enters our lives, we gain a new heart that marvels over what has been given to it, which causes us to yearn to give back! And what has been given to us?

First, we have been given *income* from the Father (Matthew 6:25–34); it is a part of the Father's generous heart to provide daily bread for us (Matthew 6:9–11). Our inflow from the Father helps us meet our material needs of food, clothing, and shelter. Yet income is just one of the many provisions the Father is actively giving us. Other provisions include *time*, *talents*, and *health*.

But by far, the most important provision from the Father is not any of these things. Rather, it is his only begotten Son—*Jesus*—and the *Holy Spirit*. They reflect the Father's perfect economy of salvation, which tasks the Son to take on flesh (incarnation) and the Holy Spirit to bring about the sanctification of God's newly adopted children (indwelling). These two provisions need to be incorporated into any Christian financial-planning model since they change everything about *how* we receive income.

As a result of the provisions of income, the Son (Jesus), and the Holy Spirit, our hearts are transformed to reflect the heart of the Father, and we become new self-giving creations. Our new hearts are generous since they are caught up in the inner life of God's generosity. Our giving is forever tied to our identity of being united to Jesus Christ and the generosity that flows within and from the Trinity (see Romans 5:5; 8:26–27, 32; Philippians 2:7–8).

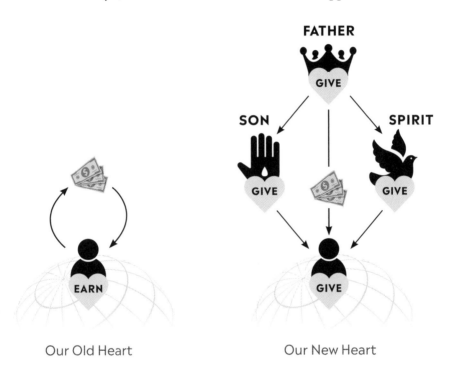

Our Old Heart   Our New Heart

Key 2: A New Mission

Before we understood the reality of the gospel, our primary mission was to earn enough to consume well. As we were immersed in our various "liturgies" of shopping and advertisements, we learned that the end goal of our lives was acquisition and consumption. Without the gospel, we subconsciously repeated the following "Costco catechism": *Our chief end is to acquire stuff so that we can enjoy it forever.*

Once the reality of the Trinity was made alive in our hearts, our new mission became to do what is most natural: love as we have been loved, and in so doing, give as we have been given to. With a heart that yearns to give, we seek to consume in ways that generously minister to others. The Apostle Paul succinctly declares our new money mission as Christians: "See that you also *excel* in this grace of giving" (2 Corinthians 8:7).

Giving is at the heart of God's character and Trinitarian nature: "God so loved the world, that he gave ..." (John 3:16). When we receive the Father's gifts of income, the Son, and the Spirit, we are equipped to show off God's generosity by giving both our material selves (time, talents, and treasures) and our spiritual selves (our unity with Christ and the Holy Spirit).

As we do this, the world gets access to the Son and the Spirit because we are "in Christ" (Galatians 3:26) and indwelt with the Spirit, becoming a part of God's economy of salvation. In other words, if we start to imitate God's generosity with all of ourselves, we become resourceful to God. He then starts to economize us to bring his salvation to the world!

New Testament scholar Craig Blomberg, who comprehensively studied all the biblical passages that reference money and possessions, found that "this principle of generosity and compassion with one's material blessings pervades the Hebrew Scriptures and applies to everyone—from the grass-roots, rural community level all the way up the social ladder to the king."[20]

The Bible contains over 2,100 instances of the word *give*, and the word *love* is used about 700 times.[21] In *The Cross of Christ*, theologian John Stott noted, "What dominated [Jesus's] mind was not the living but the giving of his life."[22] It is through experiencing the trifold blessing of the Son, the Spirit, and God's provision of income that I am set on a journey of becoming more generous, like my Father. Often my meager, stale little piece of generosity that I have to give to the Lord is all that he needs to do amazing things.

It is also very encouraging to know that I already have Jesus's generosity coursing through my blood, thanks to his completed work on the cross. The apostle Paul explained that since the riches of Christ's generosity have been given to us, we now have the generosity of Christ. John Barclay, a Pauline scholar, summarized 2 Corinthians 8:9 essentially like this: *You know the generous grace of our Lord Jesus Christ. Because he was rich [in generosity], yet for your sakes he became poor, so that by his poverty, he could make you rich [in his own generosity].*[23] After being united to Christ, I no longer need to focus on *trying* to become a generous person; instead, I'm on a journey of learning how to express the generosity I already have in Christ. We'll discuss this in greater detail in the next chapter.

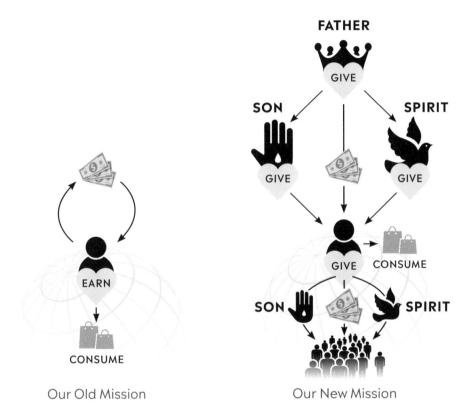

Our Old Mission   Our New Mission

Key 3: A New Vision for Saving

But if giving is so important, does that mean we are not to save or invest? The short answer is no. When our union with Christ is fully alive in our hearts and minds, we are not tempted to use saving and investing as "saviors" that attach to our identity. Instead, we use them as tools to help sustain a healthy outlet of generosity.

Before we receive the gospel, saving is a type of good that we consume in order to gain safety or greater comfort through greater future consumption. It's not necessary to try to use savings in this way, however, since the Bible states that God is the only source of true safety and comfort (see Psalm 46:1

and 2 Corinthians 1:3). Once we are a new creation in Christ, we will seek to use savings as a way of responding to God's generosity with a generosity of our own. Without savings, we can often get caught up in cycles of financial emergencies and debt. During these harmful cycles, our energy and God-given income are siphoned away to others who likely do not have our best interests in mind. This harms our ability to be generous.

Old Vision for Saving   New Vision for Saving

Savings "reservoirs" have the ability to magnify a person's ability to give throughout their life by acting in a similar way as a water reservoir, which is slowly built up over time to help a community during times of drought and fire. I personally have six months of cash as a savings reservoir, bolstering my ability to give. If I lose my job, I will not immediately have to stop giving to my church and the missionaries that we support.

My *spending plan* (which helps ensure that I spend less than I earn), coupled with a more comprehensive *financial plan* (which looks at my savings, investments, taxes, personal assets, and avoidance of debt), are tools that will allow me to sustain my giving through the inevitable hard financial seasons of life, as well as in my elder years. We will discuss creating a spending plan in chapters 4 and 5 and a comprehensive financial plan in chapter 15.

I use my spending plan and financial plan like a farmer uses his barn: to be a competent farmer. Without a barn, a farmer will not be able to survive the inevitable winter seasons. The farmer does not use his barn to stop farming but to store his resources so he can sustain his farm, produce a crop, and serve his community with the food he produces. In the same way, we can use our savings in the context of a financial plan to become more intentional with how we are going to best serve our communities.

Mimic the Sea of Galilee

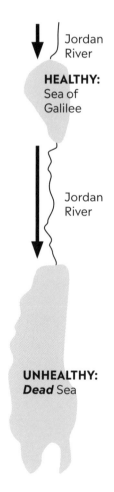

Jordan River

HEALTHY:
Sea of Galilee

Jordan River

UNHEALTHY:
Dead Sea

In the nation of Israel, there are two main inland bodies of water: the Sea of Galilee and the Dead Sea (technically they are lakes, but there was no Hebrew word for *lake* when they were named). Both are fed by the Jordan River, but one is dead and the other is teeming with life. Why the difference?

Primarily, the difference lies in whether a water outlet exists. For the Sea of Galilee, it does, but for the Dead Sea, all the water is trapped. While the Sea of Galilee freely passes on a portion of what has been given to it, the Dead Sea closes its hands on what is given, viewing all resources as scarce and accumulating them to the point where salt builds up, killing everything within the lake.

As Christians, alive in Christ, our financial lives are meant to be like the Sea of Galilee. When we use the three keys of stewardship—gaining a new heart, a new mission, and a new vision for our savings—we can then use the tools of spending plans, credit, savings, and investing to make bigger and more ambitious plans for a life of generosity. The Father's gift of our income is able to flow freely toward our community. This flow is meant to be both spontaneous and sustainable.

Because nature analogies help us more easily absorb deep spiritual truths (e.g., the Holy Spirit as wind, the kingdom as a seed), I will overlay the Trinity diagram with this Sea of Galilee nature analogy. This is a model for how a Christian should think about their personal financial planning given their identity in Christ. It is called *The Sea of Galilee Financial Model.* The purpose of providing this stylistic model is for you to more easily map out how Jesus is calling you to "excel in giving," allowing you to see all the components and realities of our finances working together for one purpose. Every person's balance between *income, savings, consumption*, and *giving* is going to look different. But the heart posture should be the same: complete and utter amazement at what we have received from the Father!

In light of the centrality of giving in whole heart finances, we need to explore what this looks like from a practical lens. For example, does "being generous" mean we give 10% of our income? In short, not necessarily. In the next chapter, we'll take a look at how our giving lives are meant to be fun, exciting, and completely a response to our identity in Christ as we receive from and share in his generous nature.

Sea of Galilee Financial Model

WHOLE HEART EXERCISES

WHERE ARE YOU NOW?

When making financial decisions, the Holy Spirit is ...

☐ Not Involved. [Mark any statements that apply.]

» I carry full financial responsibility, and it is a heavy burden on my shoulders.

» If I make a bad financial decision, I feel intense regret.

» I always feel like I'm not quite doing things correctly, and there is no one who can really help me.

☐ Intimately Involved. [Mark any statements that apply.]

» I am honored and grateful that God has given me the responsibility to help manage his money.

» I wait and seek the guidance of the Holy Spirit before I make any big financial decision.

» I am regularly looking to see how God can use my finances to bless others.

Which number best indicates the Holy Spirit's involvement in your finances?

NOT INVOLVED AT ALL								INTIMATELY INVOLVED	
1	2	3	4	5	6	7	8	9	10

PRACTICE CENTERING PRAYER

Centering prayer, a tradition that started in the early church, expresses simple truths in a way that centers ourselves on Jesus Christ. (For a more detailed discussion of this type of prayer, please read Richard Dahlstrom's excellent book *Forest Faith*.)

❏ Say the following prayers and ponder their meaning in your heart.

1. **Jesus above me:** *I receive.*

   "[Jesus] breathed on them and said, 'Receive the Holy Spirit'" (John 20:22).

2. **Jesus below me:** *I am rooted.*

   "I pray that you, being rooted and established in love, may have power, together with all the Lord's holy people, to grasp how wide and long and high and deep is the love of Christ" (Ephesians 3:17–18).

3. **Jesus around me:** *I am connected.*

   [Jesus said,] "I am the vine; you are the branches. If you remain in me and I in you, you will bear much fruit" (John 15:5).

4. **Jesus in me:** *I am called.*

   "You did not choose me, but I chose you and appointed you so that you might go and bear fruit—fruit that will last—and so that whatever you ask in my name the Father will give you" (John 15:16).

❏ The *Sea of Galilee Financial Model* provided in this chapter may seem a little abstract and hard to make your own, but the chapters ahead will equip you with the knowledge and tools you need. Chapter 15 will bring everything together so you can start to make your plan. For now, meditate on the centering prayer that follows and soak in what it is saying about who you are and your purpose with money.

1. **Jesus above me:** *I receive Jesus, the Holy Spirit, and all of God's sweet material provisions. I receive more than I could ever imagine.*

2. **Jesus below me:** *God's providential nature, through the giving of his Son and Spirit, has planted me into the deep soil of his kingdom. As his adopted child, I am truly rooted in the house of God and have been transformed to have the same giving heart as the Father.*

3. **Jesus around me:** *Jesus is on his throne, using his people in a grand plan to redeem all of creation. Through my adoption, I am connected to this kingdom and the citizens of this kingdom, my brothers and sisters in Christ.*

4. **Jesus in me:** *I am in Christ and excited to do his work with the help of the Holy Spirit. I am called into the world to be generous with what has been given to me by the Father: the Son, the Spirit, my money, my time, and my talents. I do this in response to God's love and out of a cheerful heart. I will use the tools that make up personal financial planning to bring about a greater, more sustained giving lifestyle.*

CHAPTER 3

GIVING ELEMENTS, STREAMS, SYSTEMS, AND FLOWS

The people rejoiced because they had given willingly,
for with a whole heart they had offered freely to the LORD.

1 CHRONICLES 29:9

Although I am not a naturally generous person, I am naturally curious. For me, giving is a curious thing. When I was twenty-five, I realized that giving is one of the best ways to express faith. I also saw clearly how faith was the only thing that caused Jesus to marvel (Luke 21:1–4; Matthew 8:10). My analytical brain began to do a calculation: *Giving generously equals faith, which equals Jesus's heart marveling. How intriguing—I should test this equation!* So in the name of science, I gazed at Jesus's heart and thought, *Let's get wild in my giving and see what happens.*

As I thought about what it could mean for me to "get wild" in giving, what came to mind was that I should give away my entire bonus check—about 20% of my annual salary. But there was one problem: I was headed to graduate school. I had calculated that I needed to save every bonus check and at least 15% of every paycheck in order to afford graduate school. Surely it would not be wise to get into debt.

Given that I am not a naturally wild or generous person, I decided to "put out a fleece," as Gideon did in Judges 6:36–40. He asked God to confirm his will by doing something miraculous, although in most cases, it is probably not a good idea to demand a sign from God.

My "fleece" was to ask God to give me $200 in a completely unexpected way. I don't know why I specified this particular amount; I just randomly called out a number. Within two weeks, I received two checks—one from my credit card company and the other from my utility company. Both were totally unexpected and added up to $200, so I was good to go!

I asked the Lord to put someone in my path who needed the amount of my bonus. Within a week, a friend confided that he was having trouble sleeping because of credit card debt his family had acquired from hosting a prayer conference. It just so happens that this debt was the exact amount of my bonus!

But what about affording graduate school? As it turns out, I attended a different school where tuition was much cheaper, and I was able to finish debt-free. Through this experience, I became so overwhelmed by Jesus's goodness toward me that Jesus changed my equation. Instead of "giving generously equals faith, which equals Jesus's heart marveling," I couldn't help but decide that "giving generously equals faith, which equals *my* heart marveling"!

An Outlet for Giving

As chapter 2 emphasized, our financial lives are meant to be more like the Sea of Galilee than the Dead Sea. We do this by using the three keys of stewardship: a new heart, a new mission, and a new vision for saving. We can imagine that the Sea of Galilee views its resources as abundant, so it freely gives what has been given to it. By contrast, the Dead Sea closes its hands on what it is given, viewing all resources as scarce and accumulating salt to the point where everything within it dies.

Those who are giving to the vulnerable are actually feeding, clothing, and refreshing Jesus Christ himself.

Out of the Sea of Galilee flows the Jordan River, a place God used in amazing ways. Joshua and the Israelites crossed over the Jordan into the Promised Land (Joshua 3–4), and it is also where Elijah and Elisha performed incredible miracles (1 Kings 17:1–6; 2 Kings 2), John the Baptist ministered (Luke 3), Jesus was baptized (Matthew 3:13–17), and Jesus found rest and refuge after his opponents tried to seize him (John 10:22–42).

We all can have whole hearts, where rivers of service and ministry flow outward. I personally think it's amazingly wonderful to ponder that I might serve as an outlet where Jesus Christ himself finds refuge. This is the picture we are given in Matthew 25:31–46, where those who are giving to the vulnerable are actually feeding, clothing, and refreshing Jesus Christ himself.

At this point, an important question may be rattling around inside your head: *Yes, yes, I understand that we are supposed to give, but* how much *should I give? Practically speaking, what does it mean to have a big outlet for giving?* The first way to answer this question is to address what it *does not* look like.

The 10% Box

If you ask the average Christian what it means to be generous in a practical sense, they will likely tell you, "Give ten percent" or "Tithe," which means to give a tenth of your income. Every semester, when I ask my students to create a personal financial plan, many say something like, "I am giving ten percent because that is what the Bible commands."

But a Christian who wants to be a "biblical tither" would actually need to enter into an ancient Israelite community and give three separate tithes:

1. The annual Levitical tithe (Leviticus 27:30–32; Numbers 18:21, 24)

2. The annual festival tithe (Deuteronomy 14:22–27)

3. The triannual poor tithe (Deuteronomy 14:28–29)

Adding up these three tithes would mean giving between 20–33% of their income every year. Although the tithe is mentioned twice in the New Testament (Hebrews 7:1–10; Matthew 23:23–24), it is not commanded in either of these references.

In fact, Paul is very clear that we should not be commanded in how we give money to the church: "See that you also excel in this grace of giving. I am not commanding you, but I want to test the sincerity of your love by comparing it with the earnestness of others" (2 Corinthians 8:7–8).

Academics have traced the marriage of the Christian church and the modern tithe to the Council of Tours (AD 567) and the Second

Council of Macon (AD 585), when not giving 10% to the church led to excommunication.[24]

The rule of giving 10% may also encourage a type of legalism that kills the gospel message, because it often puts Jesus in a "10% box." This box is where we give Jesus "his 10%," and thankfully we get to do whatever we want with the remaining 90%.

But as discussed in chapter 1, we do not want to live in a world where our hearts are fractured and we are not wholly baptized into Jesus. Jesus should have authority over 100% of the income in our lives.

Four Classifications of Giving

After I gave a talk before an audience where I told them the tithe lacked biblical support, a fellow faculty member asked a simple follow-up question: "If not 10%, then what? How are we supposed to know what to do if we don't follow a simple rule like the tithe?"

My answer was that a rule is immovable and unyielding, like a graveyard. It is inked on a fixed legal document. Dealing with money, on the other hand, should be more like kindergarten—filled with play and exploration.

But kindergartens are also places sometimes marked by confusion and Band-Aids, so it is much safer to simply agree that following the 10% rule is what everyone should do. Author Leanne Payne once quoted a clergyman who said, "It is much easier to preside over a graveyard than a kindergarten!"[25] Yet what the Bible teaches about giving is less like law and more like grace, where the risk of injury from less-structured play leads to the most amount of joy in that play.

Instead of defaulting to the tithe, I encourage people to think about giving as highly relational, especially when you add the Holy Spirit into the mix. Classifying giving into four different categories makes it more dynamic and fun: (1) *Elements*, (2) *Streams*, (3) *Systems*, and (4) *Flows*. As you work through these four categories, a personalized giving strategy for your household should emerge—one that goes beyond establishing a legalistic "giving law."

FOUR CLASSIFICATIONS OF GIVING

1. THREE ELEMENTS	2. THREE STREAMS	3. EIGHT SYSTEMS	4. THREE FLOWS
1. Time	1. Church	1. Firstfruits Percentage	1. Planned Giving
2. Talents	2. Community/ Neighbors	2. Increasing Percentage	2. Responsive Giving
3. Treasure	3. World	3. Firstfruits Dollar Amount	3. Untamed Giving
		4. Giving Goal	
		5. Median Household Income	
		6. Residual Percentage	
		7. Financial Finish Line	
		8. Giving Circle	

Three Giving Elements

As I seek to give using the Holy Spirit's guidance, I like to visualize having *three elements of giving*: (1) time, (2) talents, and (3) treasure. For the purposes of this book, *treasure* is defined as money and possessions. When thinking about generosity, it is a big mistake to dwell on only one of the three giving elements. Just as the Father's giving includes all three elements together (can you imagine him giving us income but not the sweet presence of his Son and Spirit too?), so our giving should seek to include all three elements together.

For example, several years ago when I lived in San Diego, I became aware of the genocide in Sudan, when Christian Sudanese were being slaughtered in the streets or forced to leave. Through my local church, I discovered there were many South Sudanese refugees living near me. I was intrigued and volunteered to transport them around the city and help them with errands.

The more time I spent with the refugees, the more I started to see how I could help them financially and with my talents in administration, writing, and video work. My wallet joyfully opened up to help these amazing people who were so full of life and beauty. As I gave my *time, talents*, and *treasure* together, I was caught up in a dynamic, joyful giving that involved all of myself.

If we give using all three elements, we will have a deeper giving life. But this may seem impossible for some of us, given our busy schedules and various demands from family and work. Simply showing up at a soup kitchen may seem overwhelming if helping in this way is not connected to your passions. We tend to make room for things we deeply care about.

Often it helps to simply find a natural fit for your giving. One way to do this is to identify the toughest time of your life. Where you have struggled is usually where you have built up an incredible storehouse of empathy for others who are also struggling in that area. This empathy creates a motivation to give of yourself. For example, if your parents divorced when you were a child, then you likely have a lot of empathy for any child whose parents are divorcing. If you were addicted to drugs, you can empathize with those who are still caught up in their addictions.

DONOR ADVISED FUNDS (DAFS)

A Donor Advised Fund (DAF) is a tool that makes giving more fun, effective, organized, and comprehensive. For more details, see wholeheartfinances.com /appendix (chapter 3).

For me, I think back to the terrible falling accident I had when I was thirteen, which forced me to spend a lot of time in the hospital. Because of this experience, I naturally want to be with others who are enduring pain in a hospital setting. I happily tend toward giving my time, talents, and treasures toward medical needs. For a period of time, I even played classical guitar at a children's hospital. However, I feel obligated to let you know that I was offering subpar talent at best!

Three Giving Streams: (1) Church, (2) Community, (3) World

The giving elements of our time, talent, and treasures then feed into the *three giving streams of our church, community, and world.* These first three streams mirror Jesus's commandment in Acts 1:8 to be his witnesses in Jerusalem (local church), Judea (community: local nonprofits and neighbors), and the ends of the earth (the world). If you are giving to only one of these streams, your vision of God's calling may become hindered. For example, just giving to the local church may limit your vision of God's love for the whole world. Likewise, giving only to local nonprofits takes away from the local church's God-given mission to be the bride of Christ.

When I think about what percentage of my giving should go toward each stream, I try not to have any laws, but rather a basic principle that guides me: *The local church should have priority over the other two streams.* I have this principle for two reasons:

1. The local church is how God the Father has chosen to bring about his salvation (Matthew 16:18); and

2. I am benefiting from what the church is providing, so there is also a certain fairness when I help fund the activities that I am benefiting from.

Given this general principle, I have a benchmark that I would like at least half of my overall giving to go to my local church. From there, I tend to split the remaining 50% in half, dedicating 25% to local nonprofits/neighbors and 25% to the needs of the world. You may have a different benchmark. When deciding on your giving-stream amounts, make sure you seek the wisdom that comes from God's Word, the Holy Spirit, and the Christian community.

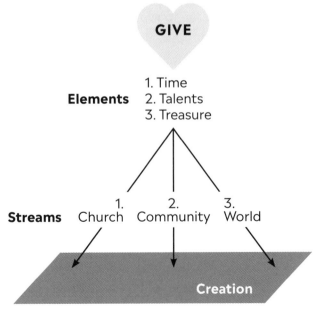

Giving Elements and Streams

In addition to the three giving streams above, our family dedicates 1% of our monthly income to a fourth giving stream called "Friends and Family" that allows us to treat them to flowers or books or a meal—just because. When we want to bless them, we don't have to break our spending plan since we've already set aside money for this type of giving. This greatly helps me since I am naturally not generous and give much more if the money has already been set aside. See chapter 5 for how you can easily set up a digital envelope that can hold 1% of your monthly income as a type of fund for treating your family and friends in a fun preplanned or spontaneous way.

Eight Giving Systems

Most people assume that within your giving streams, giving a *percentage* of your paycheck (or other forms of income) is the only way to give your treasure element. If this is your only way of giving, it will likely put too much pressure on you to find "the correct percentage."Instead, we need to consider that your giving life may benefit from adopting more than one type of giving system.

Through the years, I have identified *eight different giving systems*—ways to *structure, frame,* and *organize* your financial giving (treasure element). As I explain each system, pay attention to which one jumps out as fun or exciting, and make sure you choose one that aligns with how God has made you. Please also note that you can adopt more than one of these giving systems at a time. My family practices systems 1, 3, 4, and 6. We are also praying that we may soon participate in system 8 (Giving Circle).

1. Firstfruits Percentage

When you think "giving to the church," *firstfruits percentage* is probably what you mean. It is defined as giving a certain percentage of your income each month (e.g., 15%). The first recorded act of worship in the Bible is when Cain and Abel brought their offerings to God. A key reason Abel's offering was accepted by God was because it was considered the "firstlings" of his precious flock. Cain's offering of crops was not the firstfruits, but instead what was left over after he had kept the best for himself.

Giving our firstfruits means we give from our income before we spend it. It is more pleasing to God when we first decide what we will give before we decide how we will spend. If we spend first and then give if there is something left over, this likely leads to a heart posture where we are no longer grateful to God for our income, but instead view ourselves as the source of our income.

2. Increasing Percentage

Increasing your firstfruits percentage means using a specified standard for bumping up your giving. It could be that you increase your amount by 2% every year until it reaches 20%. Or you could increase it by 1% every time you get a pay raise.

3. Firstfruits Dollar Amount

For some, it's more practical or fun to set aside a *firstfruits dollar amount* each month (e.g., $200). This is what I did when my income was less certain. I decided to give a certain amount at the beginning of the month and then witnessed how God would provide in exciting ways.

4. Giving Goal

This is personally my favorite. I'm a pretty competitive person, and this giving system really feeds that spirit. A *giving goal* works by simply deciding how much you want to give over a certain time period. For example, I've determined a specific dollar amount I would like to give by the time I turn seventy-two. Every time I give, I am working toward this goal. And every time I reach a milestone for my goal, I throw a party!

5. Median Household Income

You decide that "the cook should not eat better than the troops" and give away any unspent income that is beyond the *median household income* of your nearest large city. For example, if the median household income is $55,000, then you would limit your lifestyle spending to $55,000 and give any amount you earn above that.

6. Residual Percentage

Give a percentage of your remaining income after accounting for expenses you need to sustain your current lifestyle. In order to protect our hearts from the dangers of giving God only what is left over, my family enjoys giving both a firstfruits percentage and a *residual percentage*. These two systems impact our hearts in different ways, so it is fun to do both.

7. Financial Finish Line

You decide the maximum amount you want to spend on your lifestyle. This amount—say, $95,000 per year—is your *financial finish line*. If you ever earn more than this amount, you will give the excess away.

8. Giving Circle

You identify a group of people with whom you want to form a *giving circle*. Everyone pools their resources, and the group collectively decides where the money should go.

Three Giving Flows

Besides having *giving systems* that structure the elements feeding into your *giving streams*, your giving will often vary in its *flow*. A healthy river's outflow is most often steady, but other times it may surge as it responds to an unexpected opening in the landscape. A deluge may even cause the river to overflow and completely overwhelm its surroundings. In the same way, you can have *three different types of giving flows*: (1) *planned*, (2) *responsive*, and (3) *untamed*.

1. Planned Giving

Planned giving is the most natural way to react to your basic identity as a believer in Christ and a recipient of all he has given you. You make a plan to maintain a steady flow of giving as a child of God who receives God's steady provision.

2. Responsive Giving

Responsive giving is when you ask the Holy Spirit to show you a specific giving plan for a specific time. This type of flow is less regular and more of a "seeking." You look around to find the little and large needs around you and then respond with your giving elements of time, talent, and treasure. Every semester I challenge my students to practice this by asking the Holy Spirit to direct them in how much money they should set aside. Next, they pray that God would put someone in their path who is in need. I always enjoy reading the fun stories that come from this assignment. Here are a few:

Student 1: "When I gave my friend the money I had set aside ($25), she hugged me and gave me a million thanks. She then shared that she was actually on her way to spend $25 on some supplies that were mandatory for her class. I was so delighted to hear this because I knew the Holy Spirit was with us and that he was still working in me and shaping me for the better."

Student 2: "I had the hardest time deciding who I was going to give $20 to, so I prayed that God would put someone in my path who needed it. When I went to San Diego this past weekend, I kept the money in my pocket hoping I would encounter somebody who needed it. When I was walking along the beach, I heard the most beautiful voice. I turned around and saw a homeless man singing and playing guitar, and I knew he was the one I should give the money to."

Student 3 (written during the height of Covid lockdowns): "I drove by my neighbor's house and put $30 in the mailbox with a letter encouraging him that everything would be okay; there were people who loved him and his family and wanted to help. Along with the $30, I gave him a bunch of toilet paper for good measure. A few hours later, he and his wife were crying when they called to express how thankful they were. They said the timing was perfect, because they were going to run out of toilet paper that evening and hadn't been able to get any from the store."

3. Untamed Giving

Untamed giving crafts amazing adventure stories. Like in the story of Mary anointing Jesus with expensive perfume, this type of giving can cause people to get upset with you (John 12:1–8). Although culture is set against this type of giving, no one who practices it, including myself, ever has regrets.

It's something you do here and there rather than constantly. Every time I recommend it to people, I feel like an adrenaline junkie who just landed safely after jumping out of an airplane: "You've got to try it, dude! It will change your life!"

My $200 fleece story is one example of untamed giving. Last year, I realized that, while I had enjoyed multiple untamed giving experiences as a single person, Tammy and I had never purposefully implemented an untamed flow of giving as a couple. We discussed and prayed about it, and then we decided to jump out of the "giving airplane" together!

Besides having *giving systems* that structure the elements feeding into your *giving streams*, your giving will often vary in its *flow*.

The Lord soon revealed a need that would necessitate draining our car savings, which we had spent seven years building. This was not a smart thing to do—it truly was untamed. But boy, was it fun! We participated in a funding effort to help a missionary family buy a house. Today it serves as home base for their ministry and for other missionary families as well.

When this giving adventure came to a close, Tammy and I went back to faithfully putting money in our "Car Savings" digital envelope (see chapter 5 for details about using digital envelopes), but with one important difference. Because God had allowed us to participate in his providential nature, it gave us both more confidence in Jesus's nearness to us and in our faith that God is a good Father who takes care of his children well. This type of confidence is impossible to gain by listening exclusively to the wisdom of the world.

WHOLE HEART EXERCISES

WHERE ARE YOU NOW?

When giving, I feel …

☐ Taxed. [Mark any statements that apply.]

- » I am irritated when I'm reminded to give to the church.

- » I feel commanded to give.

- » I tend to forget about giving.

☐ Eager. [Mark any statements that apply.]

- » I identify with 1 Chronicles 29:14: "Who am I, and who are my people, that we should be able to give as generously as this?"

- » I see giving as a natural response to God's generosity toward me.

- » I ask the Holy Spirit to reveal ways I can share what I have with others.

Which number best indicates how you feel when you give your time, talent, or treasure?

MOSTLY BITTER									EAGER
1	2	3	4	5	6	7	8	9	10

IDENTIFY YOUR GIVING STREAMS

Because your identity is "in Christ," you receive from and partake of his generous nature. God has given you time, talent, and treasure to share by giving to three streams, using various systems and flows.

❏ **1. Local Church**

» Church name: _____

» Your treasure amount: $_____

» % of your total giving: _____

» How your time will be spent: _____

» How your talent will be used: _____

❏ **2. Local Nonprofit**

» Nonprofit name(s): _____

» Your treasure amount: $_____

» % of your total giving: _____

» How your time will be spent: _____

» How your talent will be used: _____

❏ **3. The World**

» World organization(s): _____

» Your treasure amount: $_____

» % of your total giving: _____

» How your time will be spent: _____

» How your talent will be used: _____

IDENTIFY YOUR GIVING SYSTEM(S)

❏ Choose a giving system that is connected to your whole heart—something that reflects your response to the grace of Jesus Christ in your life. You can choose more than one.

MY GIVING SYSTEM(S)

1. FIRSTFRUITS PERCENTAGE	_____%
2. INCREASING PERCENTAGE	Standard for increase: _____
3. FIRSTFRUITS DOLLAR AMOUNT	$_____
4. GIVING GOAL	$_____
5. MEDIAN HOUSEHOLD INCOME (MHI)	Amount of income I will give that is above my city's MHI: $_____
6. RESIDUAL PERCENTAGE	_____%
7. FINANCIAL FINISH LINE	$_____
8. GIVING CIRCLE	Type of need to address: _____ Potential partners: _____ My contribution: $_____

IDENTIFY YOUR GIVING FLOWS

❏ List the steps you will take toward planned, responsive, and untamed giving.

1. Planned Giving: _____

2. Responsive Giving: _____

3. Untamed Giving: _____

PART 2

SPEND WITH YOUR WHOLE HEART

Make a Budget That Actually Works

Moreover, it is required of stewards
that they be found faithful.

1 CORINTHIANS 4:2 ESV

CHAPTER 4

TRACK YOUR DAILY BREAD

It is our daily bread that we eat, not my own.
We share our bread. Thus we are firmly bound to one another
not only in the Spirit but in our whole physical being.
DIETRICH BONHOEFFER, *LIFE TOGETHER*

During World War II, Darlene Rose, a missionary in Indonesia, was placed in a Japanese prisoner camp. Her daily portions of rice porridge were not sustaining her physical needs, and her body was slowly growing weak.

She noticed that a fellow prisoner was able to snag a cluster of bananas and hide them in her dress when the guards were not looking. Darlene longed for one too. "Lord, I'm not asking You for a whole bunch like that woman has. I just want one banana.... Lord, just *one* banana."

The next day, she spoke with great kindness to the commander of the camp, whom she had not seen for a while: "Mr. Yamaji, it's just like seeing an old friend!" The commander was overwhelmed with emotion. Later that day, a guard opened Darlene's door and laid ninety-two bananas at her feet, saying, "They're yours ... and they're all from Mr. Yamaji."

At that moment, she pushed the bananas into a corner and wept. "Lord, forgive me; I'm so ashamed. I couldn't trust You enough to get even one banana for me. Just look at them—there are almost a hundred."[26]

In contrast to Darlene Rose, I rarely appreciate my daily food provisions as I should. I feel entitled to my daily coffee, sandwich, and vegetables. If I can't get them right away, credit card debt, payday loans, or even stealing are potential avenues for me to get what I need. Prayer and waiting on

God's provision are not required. Can you identify? It should not have to be this way!

An Exercise in Gratefulness

A simple regular exercise of looking and tracking our income and expenses can help us realize and express gratitude for Jesus's daily provisions. And this, in turn, allows us to grow more skilled in our role as God's stewards so we might empower our ability to be generous with our whole heart. But by "looking and tracking our income and expenses," do I mean wearing a green accounting visor while hunched over a table, spending hours writing down numbers on complicated forms? Certainly not!

As I write this paragraph, I'm drinking a nice dark coffee while engaging in my daily *looking and tracking habit*. I briefly review my checking account and credit card statements using phone apps so that it's a quick process (usually no more than *three minutes a day*). As I look, I intentionally seek to find evidence that God loves me and provides for me and my family. During these moments, I have a front-row seat to witness how God truly provides for our daily bread.

I categorized my $85 electric bill as a "utilities" expense, and it prompted me to reflect on how grateful I am that God provides electricity to keep my family's food cold and fresh. I'm also grateful for the moments when his provision is for a burger instead of bread, as I just categorized a $29 family meal at In-N-Out Burger as a "restaurants" expense. It is also such an incredible privilege to own a car, and paying for the $200 annual registration is evidence of God's great provision for us to go to work, the beach, the mountains, and so many other fun places in a relatively cheap way. Thank you, Jesus!

> **THE LORD'S PRAYER**
>
> Our Father in heaven, hallowed be your name, your kingdom come, your will be done, on earth as it is in heaven. Give us today our daily bread. And forgive us our debts, as we also have forgiven our debtors. And lead us not into temptation, but deliver us from the evil one.
>
> Matthew 6:9-13

I love to weave my daily three-minute looking and tracking habit with my daily quiet time since it pairs so well with this sentiment in the Lord's Prayer: "Give us this day our daily bread" (Matthew 6:11 ESV). As I track my expenses, I see clearly how he is answering this prayer, which ushers me into having a grateful heart. Too often it is tempting to think, *I've got that part about daily bread covered, Lord.* When we are not aware of God's provision, we view our daily bread as something that we provide—not God.

An example of this attitude was featured in a Super Bowl commercial where a man was so impatient to eat a candy bar that he ate it while he waited in line to pay. When he reached the cashier, he realized he had no money. No problem! He simply opened up a new credit card on his phone and used it to buy the candy bar that was already half-digested in his stomach.[27]

What I have learned from culture is that if I want bread, I don't ever need to ask—I'll go to the store and get it. I don't even need money since my phone will give me free money while I wait in line to pay for something that I have already jammed into my mouth. In contradiction to these cultural voices, a daily looking and tracking habit helps me slow down and recognize God's provision in everything, from food to rent to health care bills.

Let Your Spending Become Light

There are more benefits to this daily three-minute looking and tracking habit (or fifteen minutes per week, or one hour per month) than just expressing gratitude for the Father's daily bread (which would be enough on its own to justify the habit). As I simply shine a bright light on what is going on each day with my spending life, my spending "becomes light." Consider the words of the apostle Paul: "Everything exposed by the light becomes visible—and everything that is illuminated becomes a light" (Ephesians 5:13).

By contrast, anything that is not exposed to light stays in the darkness. A few months after I started regularly tracking my expenses after college, I purchased a new computer and got caught up in the moment. I said yes to every possible upgrade, and the computer ended up costing twice the amount I expected.

As I sat down to log the expense, I had a moment when I desired to simply forget it ever happened. I wanted it to "go dark" and not be tracked so I would not have to deal with my shame. Thankfully that thought passed, and I logged the huge expense into my money-tracking app. As I did, my behavior was completely exposed to the light, and I felt a strong conviction from the Holy Spirit that I had just wasted his precious money. As I repented, I was immediately comforted and received the Father's incredible grace and mercy.

Some may argue that looking and tracking income and expenses is not a natural nor a healthy habit. Robert Frost, a champion of American rugged individualism, wrote a poem called *Money*, about how distasteful tracking is. Frost strongly suggested that nobody should ever "ask of money spent."[28] But when I sit down to track my income and expenses, I am making a strong statement that I disagree. I want to clearly demonstrate to myself, to Jesus, and to my community that I take seriously the role God has given me to steward his money.

As discussed in chapter 1, Jesus—who eats, drinks, and still has a material body—loves that we spend money to serve *our* material bodies, because it is what we were made to do. Being transparent is mostly about celebrating the Lord's provision and then honestly asking the Holy Spirit to bring conviction if anything we're doing is not in line with his heart.

In one of my financial planning classes, I demonstrate my belief in stewardship and transparency by completing my looking and tracking habit in front of my students. I tell them that every spending decision is connected to all people, so we should manage in a way where we could show anyone what we're doing with a clear conscience. They get to see exactly how my family is spending money as I give them an explanation of every expense. The more I show others my finances, the more the Lord can search my heart.

For example, I set aside $25 a month for going to Taco Bell once a week. This may not be something that everyone can do with a clear conscience, but each time I have brought this expense to the Lord, I have not felt an uncomfortable stirring from the Holy Spirit. Perhaps one day the Holy Spirit will stir my doctor to convince me to stop going!

Having a clear account of what we have done with God's money maps nicely to Jesus's call for us to manage worldly wealth in an honest, faithful way. Jesus says in Luke 16:11, "If you are untrustworthy about worldly wealth, who will trust you with the true riches of heaven?" (NLT). A part of being true and faithful in managing worldly wealth is to simply *shine a bright light* on what we are doing through tracking our finances. Then our spending becomes a light. And unlike Robert Frost's complaint that it is too hard to remember how we spend money, we have access to money-tracking apps and software that make "remembering" incredibly easy as these services automatically import our financial transactions (see end of chapter for more details).

Spend Less than You Earn

Besides worshiping the Lord for providing daily bread and demonstrating a clear stewardship of God's money, the third benefit that accrues to any Christian who regularly tracks their expenses is that it helps them spend less than they earn. According to a nationwide financial capability study, *only 43%* of Americans spent less than they earned each month.[29] It is much easier to spend *less* than you earn when you are keeping an up-to-date account of what you are doing.

Keeping track of your daily income and expenses is *not* budgeting. *Budgeting* is attempting to restrict your spending to a certain predetermined amount. Even if a person puts in all of the time and effort of looking and tracking, they may still fail in their budget. There are so many things out of our control that can blow up our spending plans (i.e., budgets), like car accidents or short paychecks. With looking and tracking, success is simply whether or not we do it, not whether or not we spend less than we earn, which can be almost impossible sometimes during emergencies.

As I look and keep track of my expenses each day, I am given critical information that helps me see whether I am going to outspend my income. A looking and tracking habit acts as a type of sentry at the gate who looks for signs of threats in the distance. For example, one time I noticed a $69 subscription charge for a music service that my five-year-old, Sage, had ordered when she learned how to talk to Alexa. I also noticed an incorrect late fee of $80 on my credit card and that I had spent more than I usually do on fast food. Within fifteen minutes, I was able to clear all the charges and decide to cut back on fast food. I saved over a hundred dollars during that one tracking session. Put another way, my sentry saw the angry "money mob" charging at me from a distance and pulled up the drawbridge before they were able to burn down my spending plan.

Exploring Tracking Systems

For any steward of someone else's money, the most basic requirement is to keep an account so the owner can see how their resources are being managed. Keeping an account of your hundreds of yearly financial transactions is done by first looking at what you have done, then tracking (or writing down) these expenses and, finally, placing them into spending categories. The basic goal of any *tracking system* is to produce a simple chart that shows a clear picture of what percentage of your paycheck goes toward specific expense categories (see the chart below for an example).

EXPENSES THIS MONTH

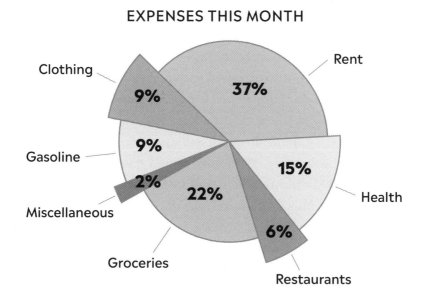

In many ways, this is a spiritual exercise, because God has given us the job of stewarding his money. Our steward role does not require a business degree or special expertise—just a little bit of time to look and track, which is both simple and highly objective. It is important to have some objective accounts of our walk with Jesus. We can worship the Lord with our mouths, but an accurate report of our expenses is a mirror into what we are truly worshiping. As Matthew 6:21 says, "Where your treasure is, there your heart will be also."

Once your expenses have been tracked and categorized, you can then show your owner (Jesus) where your money has gone for any given time period. Following are some helpful tracking tools that will allow you to keep a clear account and shine a bright light on your financial life so it becomes light. As you read about

> What then can a man do that is utterly reliable? Arithmetic! ... One plus one is two in heaven and earth and hell.... Accounting is the reckoning of facts, not fancies.
>
> Watchman Nee,
> *The Normal Christian Life*

these options, you can also reference wholeheartfinances.com/appendix (chapter 4) for helpful suggestions and supplements.

Phone Apps

For most of us, tracking is too overwhelming to accomplish by hand. *Money-tracking apps*, however, allow you to track quickly and efficiently by automatically importing transactions from each of your financial institutions (bank accounts, credit cards). This automatic process is a tremendous convenience and time saver. If you still prefer to enter this information manually, however, apps usually offer that option.

Once your financial transactions have been imported, you can place them in spending categories that make sense to you (for example, our family has three spending categories for food: groceries, restaurants, and fast food). Then a spending chart can be produced (no technical skills required), and you can share it with Jesus, an accountability partner, or your family.

One of the best features of a phone app is that your loved ones can log in as well, allowing you to stay on the same page as you track your money. Throughout the month, both my wife and I spend a few moments each day using the app to track our expenses. Phone apps also allow you to use your web browser if you do not want to do this process on your phone. I primarily look and track on my web browser, but my wife primarily looks and tracks on her phone. We are on the same team, sharing all the same information.

A myriad of money-tracking apps are available, including some with helpful personal-finance content for Christians. Some apps are free, and others require a small monthly subscription. Often if the app is free, it will not allow you to automatically import transactions or will limit how many spending categories you can create. I strongly recommend that you pay for the full services of a money-tracking app. The monthly fee is usually half of a streaming subscription. Whatever my family has spent on fees has been returned tenfold by making us much more organized in our spending, which saves us so much money every year. Another reason to pay for a service is that you will more likely use it.

Spreadsheets and Software

You can also manually keep track of income and expenses using a *spreadsheet* or *money-tracking software*. I like using a spreadsheet in addition to my money-tracking app. Once a month, I export my app data into an Excel spreadsheet, where I am able to calculate a plethora of custom financial ratios to track my financial health. A step-by-step video of how to do this is in the online appendix (chapter 4).

Paper

Using a *paper* system to manually keep track of your income and expenses is highly effective for some people, but not for others.

● ● ●

When you are in Christ, a big part of excelling in giving is to manage your daily expenses so the cost of your lifestyle fits within your income. Not managing your daily expenses often leads to overspending and a lower capacity to give. When managing your daily expenses, refrain from going straight to restricting your expenses (i.e., creating a budget). Instead, begin with a posture of gratitude through simple looking and tracking. Using an app or an alternative method, pay attention to how God is providing your daily bread. As you shine a bright light on your expenses, you will notice any problematic patterns and have the opportunity to be prayerful, acting as a faithful steward of God's money.

WHOLE HEART EXERCISES

WHERE ARE YOU NOW?

When it comes to spending money, I am ...

☐ Reactive. [Mark any statements that apply.]

» My spending is disorganized.

» I am always worried about my spending.

» I tend to overspend.

☐ Proactive. [Mark any statements that apply.]

» My spending is planned.

» My spending tends to be enjoyable.

» I tend to underspend.

Which number best describes your spending?

MOSTLY REACTIVE									MOSTLY PROACTIVE
1	2	3	4	5	6	7	8	9	10

TRACK YOUR MONEY

Tracking your money is a spiritual discipline that helps cultivate a grateful heart, faithful stewardship, and greater financial resilience for the sake of greater sustained generosity. Success is only a matter of whether you put in a small amount of time, not whether you are able to restrict your spending. And as it so happens, the more you shine a light on your spending, the more you will naturally restrict your spending.

❏ Choose your tracking system. See wholeheartfinances.com/appendix (chapter 4) for an up-to-date list of options.

» App: _____

» Spreadsheet: _____

» Money-Tracking Software: _____

» Paper

» Other System: _____

❏ Set up your tracking system so it is ready to go for next month.

❏ I will regularly track my income and expenses ... (Mark all that apply.)

Daily   **Weekly**   **Monthly**

❏ As you begin tracking, pray the following liturgy from *Every Moment Holy*.[30]

LEADER: O God Who Does Provide
All Things Necessary for Our Lives,
PEOPLE: *Be present with us now....*

For there is little in this life that will so starkly reveal
our insecurities and our struggle to trust your tender care
as will the state of our hearts when we consider
the state of our finances—
When we are anxious about money, O Lord,

we can slip so easily into the downward spiral of believing
that simply having more of it would guarantee our security.

As if our security could ever rest anywhere outside of you, O God.
So guard our hearts against that lie.
Let us learn to view money and all material things as an arena
in which to learn and practice a more faithful stewardship,
and as a means by which to invest in things eternal—
but never as ends in themselves....

Month-to-month you are teaching us—
in this paying of bills—the slow vocation of trust.
Do not abandon us to our anxieties over finances, O Lord,
but use those worries to turn our hearts and thoughts to you—
then teach us both a greater contentment
and a greater confidence in your constant care.

Amen.

CHAPTER 5

PLAN YOUR RUN RATE WITH JESUS

Here is an equation worth remembering:
Five dollars earned minus seven dollars spent = Unhappy Life.

JON MORRISON, *LIFE HACKS*

Imagine that a father decides to give his twenty-one-year-old son the responsibility of managing part of the family business. The father sits down with his son and explains that $10,000 will be given to him every month.

Six months pass, and the father calls the son into his office and asks him what he has done with the family money. The son is surprised by the question and sulks a bit. Without raising his eyes, the son quietly confesses, "I don't know." The father is shocked. "How can this be?" he exclaims. The son shrugs and says, "I'm sorry, Dad. I just haven't been keeping track."

How do you think the father will respond? Will he immediately cut off his son from future management of the family business? This response would be justified. However, that is not what our Father in heaven would do. He would tell Jesus to cook this man some fish!

In Matthew 16:18–19, Jesus reveals to Peter that he will be responsible for leading Jesus's church. Yet before Jesus was crucified, Peter denied that he knew Jesus—not once but three times! In spite of this betrayal, the newly resurrected Jesus made Peter a hearty fish fillet to reassure him that his job description had not changed (John 21:7–19).

Like Peter, we are all given responsibility over something that belongs to Jesus and the Father, including our money, possessions, time, and talents. Of course, Jesus and the Father want us to be skilled in our management of their stuff. However, just because we have this responsibility does not mean our relationship is dependent upon our performance.

We should always remember that our money and possessions are more like an allowance, and our most important job title is not regional director or head engineer but *child of God*. A parent does not give an allowance so that later they can give a "360 review" to determine their level of love for their child.

We have a smiling Dad who seeks to grow us up by giving us the responsibility of managing his stuff. And when we fail big-time, like Peter did, the warmth of Jesus's smile immediately draws us closer to the fire where he is cooking some delicious fish.

Learn from the Business World

Many people I've met have an instant, visceral response to the word *budget*; their look of despair tells me they have already tried, and failed, to restrict their spending, so what is the point? In order to avoid triggering too many people, I tend to prefer the term *spending plan* instead of *budget*. The primary reason spending plans fail is because people do not first look at and track their expenses with a heart of gratitude and stewardship (see chapter 4). Doing this first, over a long period of time before you try to restrict your spending, will give you all the correct information and motivation for a well-informed *spending plan*.

Each of us has been given access to our Father's assets as we earn income and acquire material things. If you are simply keeping track of your expenses and bringing your spending reports before the Lord, you are truly acting as a trustworthy steward of God's money and expressing your whole heart as a believer who is united to Christ.

However, there is even more that can be done. Over the last 4,000-plus years, business managers have become highly skilled at handling worldly wealth. Why not learn from the tools they have developed? One that I will teach you in this chapter is called a *run rate expense*. This is how much it will cost a business to operate in the future and includes both *regular* expenses, like payroll and cost of materials, and *irregular* expenses, such as replacing machinery.

Incorporating irregular expenses into a business plan is critical. When businesses do this, they become more sustainable. For example, the moment a business buys equipment (an irregular expense) is the moment they start saving to replace it, adding this irregular expense to their run rate. Saving for things that inevitably need to be replaced is a smart financial technique and common business sense. And yet normal households do not take advantage of this tool.

> **The primary reason spending plans fail is because people do not first look at and track their expenses with a heart of gratitude and stewardship.**

Any business that knows their run rate is able to operate more successfully since they can determine whether future sales projections will exceed their expected run rate expense. If sales are expected to be less, a savvy business manager will seek to raise more capital or cut costs to avoid going into debt.

Forgetting the Most Important Expenses

My favorite children's author is Mo Willems. I particularly like his book *Let's Go for a Drive!* In this story, Elephant declares, "Let's go for a drive!" and begins to list everything he'll need for a drive with Piggie. A map? Piggie gets one. Sunglasses? Piggie retrieves them. After fetching a few more items, Elephant suddenly has a moment of clarity as he remembers, "WE NEED A CAR!" Sadly, Piggie and Elephant do not have a car, so they are unable to go for a drive.[31]

We are like Elephant and Piggie when we do not consider every important expense for our daily living. Elephant and Piggie hilariously made plans for a drive without factoring in that they needed a car. Too often we, unfortunately, make a spending plan that does not factor in what we really need for our lives.

When making spending plans, we are great at listing regular expenses, such as groceries, rent, and utilities, and checking to see if they are less than our monthly paycheck. If so, we declare we're good to go! But we don't realize that we have left out crucial expenses such as furniture, computers, and yes, a car (or replacing the car we're currently driving).

Another basic example is replacing your shoes. When you calculated your income relative to your expenses, your shoes probably were holding up great. As time passes, however, you will likely look down and suddenly realize your shoes are tattered and need to be replaced. But if paying $40–$100 for new shoes is not in your spending plan, you will have to scramble to figure out how to get that money.

Every June, my wife and I replace our running shoes. This could be an irritating process where we might need to dip into our savings. However, for us it's fun since we've already set aside $10 from every paycheck into a special "Running Shoes" digital envelope. As June approaches every year, we have the exact amount we need without feeling guilty or scared about the financial consequences. Most money-tracking apps have this special type of "digital envelope" for setting aside specific amounts for specific purposes each month. They make it very easy to save for irregular expenses every time you get paid.

The Marsh Effect

When you do not slowly set aside money into envelopes (digital or physical) for basic things like furniture or shoes, your financial life lacks resilience. And a financial life without resilience is like a lake that has no marsh, which buffers the lake from floods and droughts.

I was a competitive swimmer in high school and still swim regularly today. It's always a great treat to swim in an open body of water, and one of my favorites is Hume Lake, located in the southern Sierra Nevada mountains. It has a dam that lets out just enough water to keep the lake at a nice full level.

But Hume Lake doesn't have a substantial marsh. One particular summer week, the city accidentally left the dam wide open, and more than a third of the lake's water drained out overnight. I didn't realize the implications before I swam the next morning. The water level was so low in certain parts that I actually got stuck in the lake weed. I was so entangled that a boater had to rescue me!

When a lake does not have a marsh and experiences unexpected water loss, everyone who relies on it suffers. Likewise, when we don't factor all our lifestyle expenses into our spending plan, any unexpected shocks that drain our income and savings will wreak havoc, leaving us stuck in slimy "debt weed." As we determine our run rate by including our irregular expenses in our spending plans, our lives gain a *financial marsh* that acts as a buffer against getting into debt during low-income droughts or big-expense emergencies.

A Full Reckoning

How much does your lifestyle cost? What is your run rate? One helpful experiment to help answer that question is to lie in bed at night and think about all the things you used, touched, and consumed throughout the day. All of these are likely needed to sustain your lifestyle, and the cost of replacing them should be incorporated into your true cost of living.

For example, if I first recall that I woke up in a bed, "bed" becomes the first item that I need to include in my run rate. A bed does not last forever, and it costs money to replace. Also, I need to think about sheets, pillows, and evening wear. These all wear down and require money to replace.

Hopefully you're starting to get the picture: Whatever things you regularly use, whether shoes, beds, coffee pots, or microwaves, you must fully reckon the cost of both using them and replacing them. Then you can determine if you are spending more than you earn over a long period of time. If you do not include these irregular lifestyle expenses, your financial life will lack resilience from sudden big purchases that were, in the end, highly predictable.

Reckoning the cost of your lifestyle is a critical part of developing your overall spending plan. Let's go over the steps you can take to create a spending plan that is fun and effective:

1. Determine your expected income.
2. Seek the Lord to determine what type of giving he is inviting you into.
3. Determine your run rate.
4. Adjust your run rate expense to accommodate your savings goals.

It begins with your expected income, then flows to your expected giving, which is something your household determines before you look at your expenses. As mentioned in chapters 1–3, giving is not something you *do*, but is inherent in who you *are* now that you are in Christ, the most generous person in the universe. It is important that your giving is your first consideration in a spending plan—something that is between you and the Lord. After all, God's giving is the whole reason you have income in the first place.

Once you have decided your giving amount in an attitude of grace and freedom, you then reckon the cost of your lifestyle using your run rate expense. Lastly, you adjust your run rate to accommodate your savings goals (a higher run rate means less savings and a lower run rate means higher savings). Your spending plan then gets put into the context of an overall financial plan, where ultimate priorities are determined—see chapter 15 for more details.

Whatever things you regularly use, you must fully reckon the cost of both using them and replacing them.

Regarding run rate (step 3), recently the US Bureau of Labor Statistics showed an average annual household expenditure of roughly $42,000 (excluding savings and charitable giving).[32] This equates to roughly $3,500 per month for the average family to maintain their lifestyle, though actual spending will vary each month since it includes irregular expenses (e.g., car replacement, paying the plumber, going on vacations).

A monthly run rate turns our cost-of-living expenses into a monthly subscription number. Our minds naturally like to think of expenses as monthly costs since many of our regular expenses like housing costs and utilities are due monthly. Marketers have realized this, and now many of the items we consume, from phones to software, are monthly subscription amounts instead of one-time purchases.

So, how do you go about calculating your monthly run rate expense (i.e., monthly subscription amount)? You begin by adding up your regular monthly expenses that are clearly charged to you, such as rent, groceries, and insurance. Then you convert your irregular expenses into monthly subscriptions.

For example, if you pay a yearly car registration fee of $100, divide this annual amount by 12 to get a monthly run rate of $8. If you want to replace your bed every ten years and prayerfully decide that $800 is the amount you want to spend, then this ten-year cost would be converted to a monthly run rate of $6.67 (if the cost of the bed will go up over time because of inflation, then you would need to use an inflation-adjusted amount such as $1,200).

Trying to account for these items can seem overwhelming, but try to generalize as much as possible. See the run rate worksheet at wholeheartfinances.com/appendix (chapter 5) for helpful suggestions. Once you calculate your run rate using the worksheet, you can take your spending plan to the next level through (1) digital envelopes, (2) sustainability calculations, and (3) Holy Spirit guidance. This combination works toward creating more financial resilience for you and your household.

Create Digital Envelopes

Now that you have converted your regular and irregular expenses into monthly numbers, you're equipped to create *digital envelopes* for every spending category. With each paycheck, you can set money aside for these expenses. These digital envelopes are easily created and managed within most money-tracking phone apps.

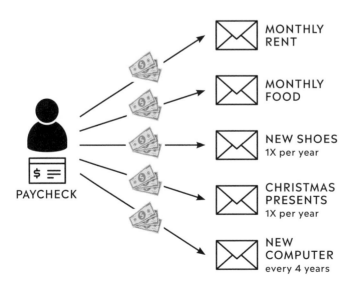

For example, if you need to save $12 per month to replace your running shoes, your next step is to use your money-tracking app, spreadsheet, or software to place $12 of your total monthly income into a digital envelope called "Running Shoes." That way you'll have $144 at the end of each year, ready to spend on running shoes. The same is true for every other type of expense you may have. For example:

Furniture
- Replace couch, bed, chairs, and table every ten years, costing a total of $4,000
- Monthly run rate = $4,000/120 = place $33 into a "Furniture" envelope every month

Vacation
- Two weekend trips ($1,000 total) and one summer trip ($1,500) every year
- Monthly run rate = $2,500/12 = place $208 into a "Vacation" envelope every month

E-Reader
- Replace every five years, costing $120
- Monthly run rate = $120/60 = place $2 into an "E-Reader" envelope every month

I personally have a lifestyle expense called "CCC," which stands for "Creeping Car Crud." When you own a car, bad things just happen. While it is impossible to know what will occur, I have been pretty accurate in predicting that one bad thing will happen every four years and will likely cost around $3,000, which means I set aside $62 into my "CCC" virtual envelope every month ($3,000/48 months).

A few years ago, when a good friend of Tammy's was visiting, Tammy asked me to go to the store to get some food. "Sure!" I said, then proceeded to back out of our garage, straight into her friend's car. Although this was a troublesome moment for me and Tammy's friend, it was not a financially hard moment. I had a few thousand dollars set aside for this very kind of "bad thing." I could have never predicted that this exact event would happen (truly a "creeping car" event!), but I can predict that something expensive is going to happen every couple of years with my car.

As you set aside money into digital envelopes, it will be tempting to spend it on other things. One helpful trick is to name your envelopes both personally and specifically. The more personal and specific the name, the less likely you will "invade" that envelope to pay for other expenses, because each envelope will become a part of who you are. The reason this is true is connected to endowment theory, which assumes that people tend to put much more value on things they have named and identified as part of their personhood (i.e., your endowment).[33]

For example, if you name your digital envelope "Savings," you will likely have no attachment to it and will view it as something you can access anytime you want. However, if you name that same envelope "National Parks Vacation" or "Mexico Vacation," you are much less likely to use it for other expenses because you're visualizing going camping or enjoying the beach.

Calculate Your Sustainability

After creating digital envelopes for your regular and irregular expenses, your next step is to see whether the monthly cost of your lifestyle exceeds your monthly income. You can *calculate your sustainability* using the following equation:

$$\text{REQUIRED MONTHLY SALARY} = \frac{\text{Monthly Run Rate}}{(1 - (\text{Tax Rate} + \text{Giving Rate}))}$$

Your *tax rate* is the percentage of your monthly income that you pay in taxes, and your *giving rate* is the percentage of your monthly salary that you donate to charitable causes. If you are having trouble finding your tax rate, look at your latest pay stub and divide *the amount of taxes taken out* by *your income before the taxes were taken out* (i.e., gross income).

Make sure you add your tax and giving rates together first before you subtract from 1. For example, if you calculate that (1) your monthly run rate is \$3,500, (2) your tax rate is 25%, and (3) you give 12% of your salary, then your calculation would look like this:

$$\frac{3,500}{(1-(.25+.12))} =$$

$$\frac{3,500}{(1-.37)} =$$

$$\frac{3,500}{.63} = \$5,555 \text{ per month}$$

If you're earning less than \$5,555 per month, then you are in trouble. It may not seem that way since most months you likely have money left over, but important irregular costs are just around the corner that will drain you.

Seek Holy Spirit Guidance

Another benefit of calculating your monthly run rate is that it helps facilitate good conversations with your loved ones, including Jesus, friends, and family. When you discuss your run rate with them you are given yet another opportunity to become fully transparent about how you are living as God's steward.

For example, after the Apple Watch came out, I waited a year before I purchased one. First I prayed about whether I should change my lifestyle since it would cost \$400, and I estimated it would need to be replaced every three years. This meant my monthly run rate would go up by about \$11 a month (\$400/36 months).

My first consideration was whether I had an extra \$11 a month to spare in my spending plan. The other more important consideration was asking the Lord for wisdom and guidance about how to best spend and use his resources, for his glory. While I don't know for sure whether it is God's will for me to have an Apple Watch, I love taking seriously my role as a steward of his money and involving him in every financial decision I make. By doing this, I draw nearer and nearer to my Lord, Jesus Christ.

Without knowing your run rate, you're never able to fully know, and own up to, your true lifestyle. Tammy and I pray about our run rate every year and seek the Holy Spirit's guidance for how we are meant to live. Honesty and transparency in our money life will bring about thriving, whereas keeping it in the dark will stunt our growth. I encourage you to pray the following prayer with all honesty, using your run rate number to help facilitate the conversation between you and the Owner of all things:

> *Search me, God, and know my heart; test me and know my anxious thoughts. See if there is any offensive way in me, and lead me in the way everlasting.*
>
> PSALM 139:23–24

Enjoy Full Resilience

Full resilience in our financial life equals combining a looking and tracking habit with a run rate that does not exceed our monthly salary. As we set aside our lifestyle expenses into digital envelopes every month, we are "tilling the soil" of our generosity. Avoiding debt and sustainably living within our means prepares us for sustained generosity. It is for the joy of giving that we make spending plans in this way.

For example, if you are in line with the median US household, then $3,500 a month is your run rate, and a relatively large percentage of this spending is setting aside money into digital envelopes. As you do this, you're in a better position to replace your car every ten years and your computer every five years, manage unexpected car repairs without any financial trouble, replace your kitchen appliances when they break down, go on fun vacations, and so much more.

All of these savings envelopes also act as a natural emergency fund, which is a critical barrier (i.e., financial marsh) that helps us avoid future debt. And this will, then, cultivate a more active, generous lifestyle. Finally, we get to pray together about whether our lifestyle is in line with what is necessary for our family to go about its mission: to love Jesus with our whole heart.

WHOLE HEART EXERCISES

WHERE ARE YOU NOW?

My daily spending is ...

❑ Unsustainable. [Mark any statements that apply.]

- » I spend first, then find money later.
- » I dip into my savings often.
- » I do not pay my full credit card balance.

❑ Sustainable. [Mark any statements that apply.]

- » I plan first, then spend.
- » I save to replace things that wear out.
- » I have set money aside for financial emergencies (i.e., emergency fund) since I expect the unexpected to happen eventually.

Right now, how sustainable are you in your spending?

MOSTLY UNSUSTAINABLE								HIGHLY SUSTAINABLE	
1	2	3	4	5	6	7	8	9	10

CREATE A SPENDING PLAN

The goal of a spending plan is to spend less than you earn to create margin and resilience for your household. Most people begin by making plans to restrict their future spending. But without looking or tracking first, the motivation and the knowledge is not available, so failure is inevitable.

Before you attempt to create the spending plan below, which involves setting limits on your spending, establish a looking and tracking habit that will give you a rich understanding of how you spend money and cultivate a heart of gratitude for God's daily bread.

❑ Building on your gratitude for God's daily provision, create a spending plan by putting money into digital envelopes, or at least begin to determine how much money will go where each month. The steps below will help you get started.

1. Calculate your expected income for the year, then divide by 12: $_____

2. Using the concepts in chapter 3, determine your expected giving for this next year, then divide by 12: $_____

3. Complete the run rate worksheet at wholeheartfinances.com/appendix (chapter 5).

4. Summarize the results of the worksheet below:

TRUE COST OF LIVING
(REGULAR + IRREGULAR EXPENSES)

1. HOME	$_____
2. AUTO/TRANSPORTATION	$_____
3. INSURANCE	$_____
4. FOOD	$_____
5. PERSONAL CARE	$_____
6. KIDS/PETS	$_____

7. HEALTH/FITNESS	$_____
8. ENTERTAINMENT	$_____
9. OTHER	$_____
TOTAL MONTHLY RUN RATE:	$_____

5. Calculate your required salary to sustain your current lifestyle:

$$\text{REQUIRED MONTHLY SALARY} = \frac{\text{Monthly Run Rate}}{(1 - (\text{Tax Rate} + \text{Giving Rate}))} = \$_____$$

6. Is your current monthly salary **higher** or **lower** than the amount you just calculated? If it is lower, then your income does not support your lifestyle over a long period of time.

7. Pray about your run rate and ask the Holy Spirit to give you clear guidance about whether you should spend more or less money on any particular lifestyle expense.

8. Add a monthly amount that goes toward savings (part 4 will help you determine what savings goals may be appropriate for you).

SPENDING PLAN SUMMARY

MONTHLY INCOME	$_____
MONTHLY GIVING	$_____
MONTHLY RUN RATE	$_____
MONTHLY SAVINGS	$_____
LEFTOVER MONTHLY INCOME (SHOULD BE $0)	$_____

CHAPTER 6

THE BLESSING OF TIRES AND ROOFS

*Even if I knew that tomorrow the world would go to pieces,
I would still plant my apple tree.*

ATTRIBUTED TO MARTIN LUTHER

One beautiful spring morning, the neighborhood birds took our door wreath hostage. They were singing their cheerful songs as usual, but two sparrows kept buzzing around the house. My wife, who knew what their noisy business was all about, quickly closed off the areas around our back patio so they could not build a nest. *Go somewhere else, you harbinger of bird poo.*

One week later, I saw a sparrow frantically fly away when I opened our front door. I was curious why the bird was so close to our door, so I peeked at our wreath and found a masterfully built nest with five little blue eggs in it! When I told Tammy, we couldn't help but laugh. The sparrows had foiled our best efforts!

From time to time, I think about how those sparrows were not forgotten by God. Jesus said, "Are not five sparrows sold for two pennies? And not one of them is forgotten before God. Why, even the hairs of your head are all numbered. Fear not; you are of more value than many sparrows" (Luke 12:6–7 esv).

Even those adorable blue eggs—the size of a penny—were precious to God. I also think about how persistent and skilled those sparrows were in building a home for their family. They certainly overcame the resistance we gave them.

Jesus had even more to say about birds: "Consider the ravens: they neither sow nor reap, they have neither storehouse nor barn, and yet God feeds them. Of how much more value are you than the birds! ... Fear not, little flock, for it is your Father's good pleasure to give you the kingdom" (Luke 12:24, 32 ESV).

It's clear that Jesus cares about the birds. And we are of *much more* value to him than birds! Not only that, but the Father has also given us his kingdom—the ultimate place of shelter and security. Given his doting attention and bountiful provision of the kingdom, how much does it really matter what type of car we drive or home we shelter in?

And yet, cars and homes still matter. A lot. Shelter is fundamental to our physical, emotional, and mental well-being, and having reliable transportation is often the only way we can earn a livable wage. Unfortunately, car and housing costs can be a burdensome source of stress. Just like in the case of household sparrows, outside forces may come in and try to keep us exposed.

In the midst of the messy process of securing our tires and roofs, it is often easy to forget about our permanent home, which has already been given to us. It is so easy to forget, in fact, that we often get impulsive and act in ways that harm our ability to be generous over the long term.

The Stress of Leasing a Car

When I was fifteen, I got my first job. As a teenager, it was a glorious thing to eat free bean burritos while earning a paycheck at Taco Bell. I saved most of my earnings for one purpose: to buy a used pick-up truck. Over the course of a year, I saved $2,000 and bought a used Chevy S-10. It had a crack in the engine that caused coolant to leak, emitting large puffs of white smoke whenever I would step on the gas. In today's world, this would likely lead to a citizen's arrest.

After years of driving my truck, named Sandpiper, I turned the key one morning, and it didn't start. I had it towed to the shop, where the mechanic laughed and said, "This thing doesn't have enough compression to spark the spark plugs!" Put another way, my poor Sandpiper had died in its sleep.

A vehicle is amazing ... when it works. Having access to a car is a lifeline that enables most of us to earn income. But for all its merits, a car is also a spending plan buster. You may be doing everything right with your spending plan until a mechanic utters horrible words like "gasket" or "transmission." These words often cost thousands of dollars that you do not have.

For this reason, many people assume it's better to *lease* a new car that typically doesn't require major repairs. Lease payments are not out of reach for most fully employed Americans,[34] so why not avoid my story of managing a "rust bucket" car that may break down, and simply lease?

There are many reasons, actually. Most important, if you are leasing a car and lose your job, you now have a payment that you cannot afford, and you will lose your car the moment you need it the most. Owning your car leads to financial resilience, because the best possible way to find work is to drive in order to physically network and shake hands.

Car insurance is also tricky when you're leasing a vehicle. Getting into an accident is much messier and more expensive than if you owned the car. Also, you pay the highest possible insurance rates, whereas owners can choose coverage that is much cheaper.

There are many other reasons to prefer owning a car over leasing one. Owning is simply cheaper since you don't have a down payment, interest charges, or depreciation fees. The depreciation and interest combined create an implicit interest charge that is much higher than the quoted rate. For example, for a new Toyota Prius leased at $420 a month with 4.2% interest, the implicit interest cost (which includes the depreciation expense embedded in the lease amount) is 9.1% (more than double!).

Another reason is that owning requires no mileage limits or damage fees. A typical mileage limit for leased cars is 10,000–12,000 miles per year with a cost of $0.20 per mile driven over that limit. Given that the average American working adult drives about 15,000 miles per year,[35] leasers are likely paying an additional $600–$1,000 in mileage fees every year. If your friends want to drive to the mountains, you may hesitate, knowing it will cost more than just gasoline. Also, a dealer charges exorbitant fees to fix damages that may happen to a leased car. Any little scratch or ding may result in hundreds of dollars of repairs.

One example of how much more relaxing owning can be happened during my college years, when I set out in Sandpiper to go surfing with a friend. Half-awake at 5:30 a.m., I crashed the side into a fixed pole near a gas pump. My friend waited to see my reaction. When I realized the dent was not going to harm the operation of my truck, I said, "Sweet! The surf is overhead, so let's go!" My carefree reaction was only possible because I owned my vehicle.

In summary, while a person who leases may not have to worry about paying a mechanic to fix major repairs, they may experience more stress from mileage limits, car insurance hassles, damage fees, and losing your car when you lose your job. Once you pay cash for a car, it is yours to drive as much as you want, whether you are employed or not, with whatever insurance you want, as long as you want, and with as many dings as you allow.

LEASING A CAR	OWNING A CAR
• High interest fees	• No interest fees
• Newest car with more amenities	• Older car with less amenities
• Most expensive insurance rates • Insurance hassles	• Lower insurance rates • Fewer insurance hassles
• Mileage limits / Fees	• No mileage limits
• High repair fees	• Lower repair costs
• Lose car if you lose your income	• Yours to keep

The Triple-Car-Payment Pit of Despair

But what about buying a car? More than 85% of new cars in the US are financed, and on average, it takes almost six years for buyers to pay off their loans, which nationwide add up to more than a trillion dollars in car-finance debt.[36]

Whether buying a new or used vehicle, I do not recommend car loans because of how they lock buyers into a *triple-payment pit of despair.* Most people are familiar with the two payments of (1) repayment of the loan and (2) the payment of interest. However, there is a third payment that you should also consider: cash savings that will help you avoid using debt to buy your next car. This third payment applies to leased vehicles as well.

For example, if I took out a car loan equal to about $26,000, my monthly payment would amount to $470.[37] This includes the repayment of my initial loan and interest assessed on that loan. If I ever decided it would be better to avoid debt by paying cash for my next car, I would also need to save $330 each month in order to replace my car after ten years (this amount includes the cost of car prices going up over time).

> **TRIPLE-CAR-PAYMENT PIT OF DESPAIR**
>
> 1. Loan repayment
> 2. Interest
> 3. Cash savings for future debt-free car purchase

This triple payment totals $800, which is likely too much for most people. Once we have a car loan, it is simply too hard to have enough extra cash to repay the loan, pay the interest on that loan, and save for our next car so that we won't use debt in the future. It has been reported that a third of people who are buying new cars while trading in their old cars will also roll over debt from their old vehicles into their new loans, further pushing them into a vicious cycle of debt.[38]

Buy Used, with Cash

What shall we conclude, then? In general, it is best to maximize your financial resilience by purchasing *used cars* with cash. Because vehicles depreciate over time, used cars will always be available at reasonable prices. Even if special circumstances reduce supply and increase used car values (which happened after the Covid-19 pandemic), these factors will eventually return to more normal levels.

When shopping for a used car, there are many more options and tools available today than when I bought my first used car in 1996. Most car manufacturers now have *certified pre-owned* guarantees, and a CARFAX report may identify a used car that has had too many owners, accidents, or manufacturer recalls. Another good tip is to pay a trusted mechanic $100–$200 to inspect a prospective vehicle. You may have to do this a few times before you find the right car, but it might save you thousands of dollars in repair costs.

It is best to maximize your financial resilience by purchasing *used cars* with cash.

The bottom line is that owning a used car saves money over time—likely about $20,000 every ten years. This calculation includes new transmissions and tires, and it doesn't even factor in the resale value of your car after ten years and the benefit of keeping your vehicle if you were to lose your job.

Home-Buying 101

While a car is likely the first major purchase we will make after becoming fully employed, buying a home is likely the biggest purchase we will make during our lifetime. Homes are a very expensive matter, with recent median US home prices over $428,000.[39] I live in Southern California, where the current median is almost $1,000,000.[40] Because I am not a millionaire, I cannot simply "buy a home." Although I technically "own my home" at this present moment, that idea seems laughable to me. I do not really own my home; instead, I have access to it from a mortgage, with the hope that I might officially own it in thirty years.

Because homes are so expensive, there is an entire language that centers around how to purchase one without actually having the money to buy it. Allow me to define some of the most important terms you should know.

Mortgage

When a bank gives you money to buy a home, the loan is called a *mortgage*. This term comes from the Anglo-French word *mort*, which means "death," and the Middle English word *gage*, which means "pledge" or "commitment." Why is "death" included in the definition of a finance term? It was meant to convey the posture that you're binding yourself to a commitment (*gage*) where you would rather die than break your bond (*mort*). Traditionally, you were essentially entering into a "death pledge." Thankfully, today it's much less dramatic. If you can't pay back your mortgage over a fifteen- or thirty-year time period, usually you will just have to give your home keys to the bank in foreclosure. While this is much nicer than death, a foreclosure can be disastrous for your credit, causing difficulties in many areas of your life (see chapter 9).

Fixed or Variable APR

A bank will charge interest on your mortgage every month until the loan is repaid. Interest rates, although assessed every month, are required by law to be quoted in annual terms. *APR* stands for the Annual Percentage Rate of a loan. If an APR is *fixed*, the interest cost will not change over the life of the loan. If it is *variable*, the APR may change anytime.

Fixed-Rate vs. ARM

The most traditional mortgage is a thirty-year *fixed-rate loan*. This means the loan will have an unchanging, fixed monthly payment over a thirty-year period. You can get a variable APR thirty-year loan where your payment changes every year, but these types of loans are not commonly sold. A hybrid between fixed and variable APR loans is an *adjustable-rate mortgage (ARM)* loan, which is fixed for a few years and then "adjusts" to a variable rate after the initial fixed period.

The adjustment period is communicated in the first number given in an ARM description. The second number refers to how often the rate will adjust after the first fixed period. A "5/1 ARM" has a five-year fixed-rate period and then resets every year after that. A "7/1 ARM" has a seven-year fixed-rate period and then resets every year after that. People tend to like ARMs since they have much lower rates during the fixed period, but after this the monthly payment can rise substantially.

These are also dangerous products since consumers are told they don't have to worry about what the higher payment will be after the adjustment period since they can "cash in" on the money they make as their home price goes up. However, as thousands of people learned during the 2008 global financial crisis, housing prices do not always go up. Having an ARM during that time meant losing your home after the adjustment period. While those with ARM mortgages represented only 18% of all high-quality mortgages (prime) and 48% of low-quality mortgages (subprime), more than half of all the prime foreclosures and 73% of subprime foreclosures were from those with ARMs.[41]

Agent

Traditionally, a *real estate agent* has been a critical part of any home purchase or sale. If you're looking to buy, working with an agent increases the odds that you'll find the right home. If you're looking to sell, an agent increases the odds that you'll find a buyer. Perhaps the most important role an agent plays is helping both buyers and sellers navigate thousands of pages of legal documents that must be signed. A selling agent has traditionally charged about 6% of the home price as commission (this rate is dropping, though).

Down Payment and PMI

Banks do not like to lend without some sort of "skin in the game" from the borrower, so they usually require a *mortgage down payment*—cash you will provide up front. The traditional amount is 20% of the home price, which allows you to avoid paying several hundred dollars each month for *private mortgage insurance (PMI)*. PMI is another safeguard for banks since the insurance company will continue to make payments in the event you stop making yours. Having a 20% down payment also qualifies you for a lower APR and makes your home bid more competitive.

Escrow

When purchasing a home, a buyer isn't going to simply walk up to the seller with a briefcase full of cash. Instead, the agent will use an *escrow company* to receive and distribute money exchanged during a real estate transaction: agent commissions, attorney fees, loan processing fees, and property appraisal fees. On average, a buyer will pay $4,000 in fees, and only the seller pays the agent's commission.

Interest-Only (IO) Loans

Banks often carry *interest-only (IO) loans* in addition to traditional mortgages. For IO loans, every payment is applied only to interest. People like IO loans since their payments are often half of what a traditional mortgage payment would be. They are essentially "paying rent" and, if the value of the home goes up, they can cash in on that rise (i.e., equity) and potentially transition to a traditional loan.

For example, I had a friend who completed his graduate work in Scotland over a four-year period. Rentals were hard to come by, so he purchased a home using a $400,000 IO loan. When his schooling was over, his loan amount was still $400,000. At that point, if his house was worth more than the loan—say $500,000—he could sell it, pay off the loan, and then pocket the extra $100,000. However, if the home was worth less than the loan—say $350,000—he would need an extra $50,000 to pay it off (which is unlikely for a theologian).

Like ARM loans, IO loans are often predatory. Consumers are promised that home prices *only go up*, but if your value decreases, you may owe tens of thousands of dollars to the bank if you need to sell your home.

FHA Loans/First-Time Home-Buying Programs

The *Federal Housing Administration (FHA)* seeks to make housing more affordable and provides loans with lower down payments, lower closing costs, and easier credit qualifications. Mortgage insurance premiums are still required, however, and sellers may not want to work with you if they know the government is the lender. But an FHA loan may be the ticket if you cannot afford a sizable down payment. Also, local governments often have generous mortgage opportunities for first-time buyers that include qualification for a low APR mortgage, even with a 0% down payment. Ask a local credit union or commercial bank for more details (see chapter 11 for more on credit unions).

Should You Buy a Home?

Over the short term, renting will always be easier on your wallet and schedule, leaving you with more time, money, and options. Owning a home involves many hefty costs on top of your mortgage, including appliances, property taxes, homeowners insurance, water and trash bills, maintenance and repairs, lawn care, and pest control. If your mortgage is $1,500 per month, you may actually be paying more like $2,500 per month when you consider the additional costs.

In general, however, owning a home for more than a housing cycle (as long as ten years) most often leads to significant wealth gain. One of the most common questions I get is, "Should I buy a home while prices are so high?" My usual response is, "Prices are always high! That's the trade-off when there is access to lots of financing, because easy access inevitably pushes up the price of whatever you are financing."

It is usually best to buy, not when prices are low, but when you know you have a high probability of staying put through an entire housing cycle. If you buy at the top of the price cycle, your home price will mostly go down for a long period. For many who paid peak prices in 2007, their home prices plummeted for many years, finally reaching the original purchase price about thirteen years later. It's important that you resist the temptation to chase after easy money by purchasing a home when you won't likely be firmly planted in your neighborhood, career, and family life. If you buy when home prices are high, think long-term so you can weather an economic downturn.

The other important consideration when you're thinking about buying is whether you can get a prequalified mortgage. *Prequalification* means you ask a bank, or better yet, a mortgage broker, to secure a competitively rated mortgage before you put in any offers for a home. Then you are much more competitive when putting in an offer. If you are prequalified for a 0% down payment (e.g., FHA loan), you will have a harder time having a seller accept your offer since no one likes doing business with the government. If your prequalification is from a major bank and includes a 20% down payment (showing you are a serious and stable buyer), then you will have a much more competitive offer.

One of the most important hurdles for securing a competitively rated mortgage is known as the *housing ratio*—the percentage of your monthly household income that goes toward housing costs (principal and interest, taxes, and insurance). If your housing ratio is more than 30%, then you will likely either be rejected for a prequalified loan or get one with a much higher APR.

A whole heart in Christ is not hurried or worried about cars or shelter, but instead has a long-term perspective that works toward ownership.

In summary, if you are looking to buy a home, prioritize having both stable income and a solid down payment in order to have access to a competitive bid and make it through any ten-year housing downturn. In general, there are myriad exceptions to this principle, but always walk with a healthy fear of buying a home since it has the power to both create and destroy wealth so quickly.

And if you are among the large percentage of Americans who will likely never have access to a competitive mortgage because your income is too low or you cannot put together a 20% down payment, consider FHA loans and the first-time home-buying programs mentioned above. Above all, know that the Lord deeply cares about where you sleep. Like a loving Father and a good shepherd, he will look after your needs with incredible skill and thoughtfulness.

● ● ●

Cars and homes are big purchases that require complicated decisions since we often cannot afford to buy them, and yet we need wheels to get around and the protection of a roof over our head. The world has capitalized on our panic and created a web of products that allow us to acquire them even when we don't have cash to buy them. Very often, we cling to these products, thinking only in the short term.

The recommendations I've made in this chapter are meant to help cultivate a whole heart that takes seriously Jesus's words that we are seen, known, and loved by the Father, who has given us the kingdom. A whole heart in Christ is not hurried or worried about cars or shelter, but instead has a long-term perspective that works toward ownership. This creates the smoothest possible path for a life of generosity because it avoids the pitfalls of short-term, high-interest debt solutions, which siphon away precious resources the Lord has given us to manage.

WHOLE HEART EXERCISES

WHERE ARE YOU NOW?

My possessions are typically ...

☐ Borrowed. [Mark any statements that apply.]

» I don't own most things that I use—I make payments.

» If I were to lose my income, I would lose my possessions.

» I want nice things now, and I do not want to deal with used cars, furniture, or appliances.

☐ Owned. [Mark any statements that apply.]

» I own the things I use, including cars, furniture, and appliances.

» I'm okay with having used things as long as I'm saving to replace them with nicer versions.

» If I were to lose my job, I could either sell my things or use them to help me find a new job.

How much of an owner are you?

I DON'T OWN MOST THINGS I USE								I OWN WHAT I USE
1	2	3	4	5	6	7	8	9	10

MOVE TOWARD OWNERSHIP

❏ Prioritize paying for your next car with cash by establishing a "Car Savings" envelope in your spending plan.

❏ Search online home-buying sites to find a few houses you would love to purchase. See wholeheartfinances.com/appendix (chapter 6) for a few suggested websites.

❏ Calculate your housing ratio for these homes. Only pursue homes where your housing costs* are less than 30% of your monthly household income.

$$\text{MY HOUSING RATIO} = \frac{\text{Housing Costs (PITI)*}}{\text{Gross Monthly Income}} = \underline{\hspace{2cm}}\%$$

*Housing Costs = PITI = mortgage payment (Principal + Interest) + property Taxes and Insurance payments

CHAPTER 7

DISCOVER YOUR MONEY PERSONALITY

It was his habit to always have some money about him.
The mournful life to which he had been condemned
imposed this as a law upon him.

VICTOR HUGO, *LES MISÉRABLES*

During Jesus's teaching ministry, a collector of the temple tax asked Peter whether Jesus paid the temple tax. Even though he technically did not have to pay the tax because he was the Son of God, Jesus asked Peter to go ahead and pay it—in a rather strange manner: "Lest we offend them, go to the sea, cast in a hook, and take the fish that comes up first. And when you have opened its mouth, you will find a piece of money; take that and give it to them for Me and you" (Matthew 17:27 NKJV).

I love this story for two reasons. First, for how fun and creative Jesus is when paying a tax. If you were to ask someone to name their least favorite activity, their answer would likely be "Paying taxes." Not so with Jesus. A fish with a coin in its mouth is a hilarious and creative way to tackle what we think of as an unpleasant task.

Second, I love how personal Jesus is toward the individual hearts of his followers. Quite wonderfully, Jesus also relates to us with his own unique heart and personality. Because Peter was a fisherman, I think Jesus chose fishing as Peter's method for paying the tax. Since I can't fish at all, I imagine Jesus would peer into my heart, see that I love open-water swimming, and ask me to swim the seas to find a seashell with a coin in it.

Within our personalities, our hearts uniquely relate to money in ways that are both healthy and unhealthy. In the same way that our need for tires and roofs may help or hurt our spending plan (depending on whether we become too short-sighted in meeting our need), our *money personalities* have the potential to help or hurt our spending plan, depending on how our money personalities are expressed.

My two children, Sage and Silas, are very close in age and quite inseparable when they are together at home. They have their own language and games. However, they relate differently when it comes to money. When I give Sage money, she immediately stores it away, like a chipmunk. When I give Silas money, he immediately looks for ways to use it, like a playful otter.

Just as there is no correct type of personality (e.g., extrovert vs. introvert), there is also no correct type of money personality. However, money personalities *can* become distorted (often from past experiences), meaning our hearts no longer relate to money in a healthy way.[42] Over the last twenty years, psychologists have classified money personalities in several ways. I will focus on two methods—*Money Worlds* and *Money Dimensions*—so that you can get a better picture of how you naturally relate to money.

Money Worlds

Professor Miriam Tatzel, a social psychologist, was able to condense various attitudes and values about money into two primary characteristics:[43]

1. Degree of Looseness with Money

If you are *loose with money*, then you are willing, or even eager, to spend. You believe that by spending more, you will get the best. By contrast, if you are *tight with money*, you are usually reluctant to spend, and any large outlays need to be thoroughly justified.

2. Degree of Materialism

If you are *high in materialism*, you derive pleasure from material things that improve your quality of life. If you are *low in materialism*, you view material things as relatively neutral tools, and you delight more in experiences that improve quality of life.

Please note that being high in materialism is not morally wrong! It just means that God made you to particularly enjoy life through material things. A good example is a description of the main character in the novel *The Talented Mr. Ripley:*

> He loved possessions, not masses of them, but a select few that he did not part with. They gave a man self-respect. Not ostentation but quality, and the love that cherished the quality. Possessions reminded him that he existed, and made him enjoy his existence.[44]

Combining the Two

When combining these two characteristics of looseness and materialism, Professor Tatzel was able to map four possible *Money Worlds*. They look something like this:

MONEY WORLDS

	TIGHT	LOOSE
HIGH MATERIALISM	**Value Seeker** Spends extensive time researching and saving in order to buy nice things.	**Big Spender** Spends money on nice things in order to feel connected to themselves and others.
LOW MATERIALISM	**Non-Spender** Avoids spending because it is painful. Would be happy to never go shopping or have much stuff.	**Experiencer** Sees money as a way to buy experiences and services that lead to growth and development.

According to the chart, where do you fit? I tend to be an *Experiencer*, and my wife is more of a *Value Seeker*. My low materialism and looseness with money means I don't mind spending for experiences, but I don't enjoy buying things that don't involve self-development (like clothing). Tammy, on the other hand, likes nice food and wants quality items for our home, so she is willing to spend more to get these things, albeit after a lot of bargain hunting and research.

Our different money personalities had a major clash after one year of marriage, when I turned to Tammy and said, "Honey, let's spend two weeks in Europe! It will cost about $5,500, and I've already figured out where we should go!" My wife then said, "Come again? How is it that you hound me every time I spend $10 more than our monthly grocery allotment, but you are willing to spend $5,500 just like that?"

As mentioned before, one key lesson is to understand there is no "correct" money world. Each variety has both healthy and unhealthy expressions. For example, if your husband is a *Big Spender* and you are a *Non-Spender*, you will likely encounter plenty of financial conflict. A good first step is for each of you to acknowledge that both personalities are legitimate ways of relating to money.

For example, Big Spenders tend to be great at hospitality. They are naturally able to create beautiful places and comfortable spaces because of their high materialism. By the same token, Big Spenders may think there is nothing good about being a Non-Spender, casting them as cruel, Scrooge-like characters. However, the simple life of a Non-Spender can be an inspiring example to us all, like Maria from *The Sound of Music* arriving at her new home with only one bag, her guitar, and a big smile.

Money Dimensions

Another way you can identify your natural money personality is to use the framework called *Money Dimensions*, developed by Dr. Eileen Gallo.[45] This framework illustrates how we can have a unique relationship with money across three different dimensions: (1) Acquisition, (2) Use, and (3) Management. While we may exhibit all three dimensions, only one is our primary way of relating to money. For each of the three dimensions, there is also a healthy and an unhealthy way to relate to money. And within each unhealthy expression, there are two opposite ways people can be unhealthy.

Acquisition (A)

If your primary money dimension is *Acquisition (A)*, you mostly view money as a type of *collectible*. You immediately treat it like it's a game to win and believe that you can "level up" by collecting more money. Seeing the need to collect something that has value in this life is not necessarily right or wrong, but there are two ways that an Acquirer can become unhealthy. In one extreme, he or she develops an insatiable appetite to acquire money, like Smaug the Dragon from *The Hobbit*, who was cursed with an unending appetite for gold. The other extreme is to become completely avoidant of acquiring money, like a flagellant monk who sees money as a cursed collectible, occasionally leaving his cold, desolate cave to condemn people in town for enjoying their earthly attachments.

Use (U)

If your primary money dimension is *Use (U)*, you mostly view money for its potential use—as a type of *ticket* for enjoyable consumption. In your mind, every twenty-dollar bill instantly transforms into a good restaurant dish, weekend entertainment, or a pampering manicure. At one extreme, a User can become unhealthy by developing an appetite to spend. Like Cher in the movie *Clueless*, a User comes home with bags full of expensive clothing to feel better about life. The other extreme is using money as a ticket to keep you safe and secure as you restrict spending and save like a miser.

Management (M)

If your primary money dimension is *Management (M)*, you mostly view money as a *to-do* that you need to manage. Every dollar bill is a puzzle to be solved. This is exactly how my daughter, Sage, and I relate to money. You'll see a small look of pain on our faces as we figure out the best possible way to manage our cash. A Manager can become unhealthy by developing an ever-increasing appetite to micromanage everything about how money is used, spent, given, and saved.

When I am expressing an unhealthy money personality, this is how I do it. I stop being in the moment, enjoying my family, and instead, focus on achieving the perfect spending plan. I use a spreadsheet to make sure that every dollar is managed to my satisfaction, all to the detriment of my wife and kids. They become obstacles to my perfect planning, not people I am meant to care for. At the other extreme is someone who, after suffering under the rule of a micromanager, willfully chooses a hands-off approach, fearing they will harm people in the same way they were harmed in the past. This is the person who plugs their ears every time you seek to have a meaningful discussion about spending plans.

MONEY DIMENSIONS

	ACQUISITION (A)	USE (U)	MANAGEMENT (M)
DESCRIPTION	Money is a *collectible*.	Money is a *ticket* that helps you consume something you want.	Money is a *to-do* that needs to be checked-off.
SECURE	**(A)** Your acquisition desire is healthy to you and others.	**(U)** Your consumption desire is healthy to you and others.	**(M)** Your desire to manage money is healthy to you and others.
ADMIRABLE	**(A+)** You acquire money for yourself and others in an inspiring way.	**(U+)** You consume money for yourself and others in an inspiring way.	**(M+)** You manage money for yourself and others in an inspiring way.
INSECURE EXTREMES	**(A-) Insatiable:** There is always a higher wealth level you want to reach. **(A-) Avoidant:** You treat money like a cursed collectible in a way that harms yourself and others.	**(U-) Overspender:** You cannot get enough things to consume. **(U-) Miser:** You cannot get enough protection from money.	**(M-) Micromanager:** You need to control others so your spending plan will succeed. **(M-) Chaotic:** You're terrified about money hurting your relationships, so you avoid spending plans altogether.

Working through Your Money History

After identifying your money world and your money dimension, consider how you have become unhealthy in your money personality. For example, if you are a *Value Seeker*, that's great, but perhaps you sometimes seek comfort from material things instead of Jesus. Or if you have discovered that you primarily relate to money as something you *Use*, perhaps you've realized you often use money for safety and security, which robs you of receiving those things from God the Father instead.

I know that, when I am unhealthy, I go straight into *Non-Spender* mode, austere and condemning of all expenditures. I become a *Micromanager* who hovers over my wife's grocery cart. "No, not the expensive cut of meat, dear!"

But why do we sometimes adopt an unhealthy money personality in the first place? It's more than just ascribing these behaviors to our "sinful nature." The fact is that our money lives have been heavily influenced by our families and life events.

Following are two methods that can help us identify these environmental factors and better understand why we often "go off the rails" with our money personalities.

Money Genogram

When I was in middle school, I often spent time at a friend's house after school. Throughout the years, I noticed their family had a pattern. Every time my friend had any type of sadness, his mom would immediately reach into her purse, pull out some cash, and say something like, "You are a good boy, so go out and do something fun."

My friend's mom, who was trying her best to love her son, had a clear view of money as something to *Use* and likely had a money personality that was both loose and high in materialism. She likely influenced my friend's money personality in profound ways. He may have adapted his natural money personality by reacting to what his mom did, becoming very tight and nonmaterialistic, or he may have mimicked how his mom relates to money.

The Financial Therapy Association (FTA) has been at the forefront of developing useful tools for individuals who want to explore their relationship with money. One such tool is a *Money Genogram*. Genograms have been used by psychologists for decades to help people understand how they've been influenced by their family of origin. It works like this:

1. Create a family tree.

2. Note the primary money dimension for each of your family members (*A*, *U*, or *M*).

3. Designate whether you mostly experienced a healthy or unhealthy expression of this dimension by putting a plus (+) or minus (-) sign next to the letter.

For example, if my friend felt like his mom was expressing an unhealthy *Overspending* version of the *Use* money dimension, then within his mom's genogram circle he would write "U-". Following is an example of a money genogram. You will have an opportunity to create your own at the end of this chapter.

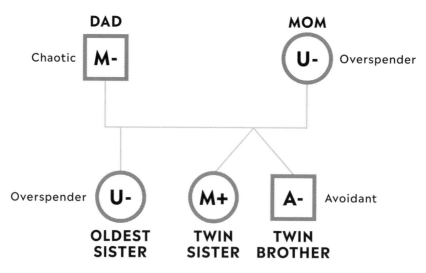

Money Genogram

Money Autobiography

The second way you can discern how your environment has influenced your money personality is to identify the life events that have influenced your views about money. It can be very helpful to create a timeline of moments and seasons when money is experienced as either pleasurable, neutral, or painful. Writing a *Money Autobiography* can help you identify possible reasons for certain triggers that instantly launch you into an unhealthy money personality.

For example, a friend once confided in me that his parents always fought over money after his dad lost his job. When my friend got married, anytime he would have a garden-variety fight with his wife (e.g., "Who's doing the dishes?"), he would instantly become terrified about their money situation, even if their finances were strong. Once my friend realized this was a trigger, he was able to lovingly convince his "six-year-old self" that their arguments were of a completely different nature than his parents' fights over money.

Healing Your Unhealthy Tendencies

Once you reflect on your money history, the best way to become healthier in your money personality is to simply move your heart toward Jesus. Just like a child learns how to eat, drink, and speak by spending time with their parents and imitating them, so we can learn how to positively relate to money by studying and imitating the money world of Jesus, which can best be described as "holy looseness" that leads to "holy materialism." In Luke 6:38, Jesus calls for a radical "holy looseness" with money when he says, "Give, and it will be given to you. A good measure, pressed down, shaken together, and running over, will be poured into your lap. For with the measure you use, it will be measured to you."

This holy looseness with money is fueled by the truth that God is the owner of all our stuff, and we are simply stewards who should respond to his abundant generosity with a generosity of our own. Many people hate this idea of being loose with money, fearing it will inevitably lead them to become an irresponsible Big Spender. This certainly won't happen, because as we are generous with God's money in response to his generosity, our materialism becomes sanctified. We gain a "holy materialism" when our enjoyment of the Giver overshadows our enjoyment of goods, which means we will only be loose with money to the extent that it helps us enjoy material things *alongside* Jesus. We do this in a way that is self-giving and makes Jesus look good to the world.

The parable of the prodigal son describes a beautiful scene where there is a holy looseness with money and a holy materialism. When the prodigal son returns, the father, in his joy, says, "Quick! Bring the best robe and put it on him. Put a ring on his finger and sandals on his feet. Bring the fattened calf and kill it. Let's have a feast and celebrate" (Luke 15:22–23). Let us move our hearts toward a holy looseness that is generous, coupled with a holy materialism that seeks to enjoy creation alongside our Savior, Jesus Christ. When we combine this with a spending plan cultivated in prayer, we become more skilled at managing God's money so that we can further excel in giving it away.

WHOLE HEART EXERCISES

WHERE ARE YOU NOW?

When it comes to my relationship with money, I am ...

❏ Unaware. [Mark any statements that apply.]

> » I make decisions with money that frustrate myself and others.

> » When people talk about money, I immediately get stressed out.

> » I can't stop spending money to feel better.

❏ Self-Aware. [Mark any statements that apply.]

> » I know what beliefs I have regarding money and how I naturally relate to money.

> » I can describe how my family has influenced my relationship with money and the triggers that cause my unhealthy money behaviors.

> » I am taking steps to express my natural money personality in healthy ways.

How self-aware are you when relating to money?

I'VE NEVER THOUGHT ABOUT IT						I KNOW HOW I RELATE TO MONEY			
1	2	3	4	5	6	7	8	9	10

IDENTIFY YOUR MONEY PERSONALITY

❏ Use the following charts to help identify your Money World.

TIGHT		LOOSE
I am reluctant to spend money, and any large outlays need to be thoroughly justified.	OR	I am willing, or even eager, to spend. I believe that by spending more, I will get the best.

LOW MATERIAL		HIGH MATERIAL
I view material things as mostly burdensome necessities.	OR	I derive pleasure from material things that improve my quality of life.

MY MONEY WORLD

	TIGHT	LOOSE
HIGH MATERIALISM	**Value Seeker** I spend extensive time researching and saving in order to buy nice things	**Big Spender** I spend money on nice things that help me feel connected to myself and others.
LOW MATERIALISM	**Non-Spender** Spending money is painful. I would be happy to never go shopping or have much stuff.	**Experiencer** I see money as a way to buy experiences and services that will foster my growth and development.

❏ Identify your primary Money Dimension using the following chart.

MY MONEY DIMENSION

CATEGORY	DESCRIPTION	Y OR N
Acquisition	Money is a *collectible* that helps me "level-up."	
• Secure [A]	My acquisition desire is healthy for me and others.	
• Admirable [A+]	I acquire money for myself and others in an inspiring way.	
• Insecure [A-]/ Insatiable	There is always a higher wealth level I want to reach.	
• Insecure [A-]/ Avoidant	I treat money like a cursed collectible in a way that harms myself and others in my life.	
Use	Money is a *ticket* that helps me consume something I want.	
• Secure [U]	My consumption desire is healthy for me and others.	
• Admirable [U+]	I consume money for myself and others in an inspiring way.	
• Insecure [U-]/ Overspender	I desire to use money to consume more and more.	
• Insecure [U-]/ Miser	I desire to use money to buy more and more protection.	
Management	Money is a *to-do* that needs to be checked-off.	
• Secure [M]	My desire to manage money is healthy for me and others.	
• Admirable [M+]	I manage money for myself and others in an inspiring way.	
• Insecure [M-]/ Micromanager	I need to control others so my spending plan will succeed.	
• Insecure [M-]/ Chaotic	I'm terrified that money will hurt my relationships, so I avoid spending plans and financial plans altogether.	

REFLECT ON YOUR MONEY HISTORY

❏ Create a Money Genogram to diagram your family of origin (see the example on page 104).

  1. Specify each relative's primary money dimension.

  2. Add a positive sign if you experienced a healthy version of that money dimension and a negative sign if you experienced a negative version.

❏ Write a Money Autobiography that captures memorable moments that influenced how you think and feel about money.

  1. Begin with your earliest memory of money.

  2. Focus on moments when a surplus or lack of money was a meaningful part of good times or hard times.

PART 3

GUARD YOUR WHOLE HEART

Relate Responsibly to Credit and Debt

Debts are nowadays like children begot with
pleasure, but brought forth in pain.

ATTRIBUTED TO MOLIÈRE

CHAPTER 8

CREDIT PREDATORS

*For him a debt was the beginning of slavery. He felt even that
a creditor is worse than a master; for a master owns only your
person, a creditor owns your dignity and can belabor that.*

VICTOR HUGO, *LES MISÉRABLES*

Sandy Hudson was short on cash one day and decided to try out her local payday shop. In only fifteen minutes, she paid an $18 fee to receive a loan for $100. However, additional unforeseen fees caused her to take out new loans to pay off her old loans, and after just six months, she owed $3,600, with no hope of getting out of the steel trap she had unknowingly stepped into.[46] Sandy was held captive.

Jesus cares for those who are prisoners not only because of their sin but also because of their hard circumstances and misguided financial choices. At the beginning of his public ministry, Jesus boldly proclaimed he was fulfilling these words that Isaiah the prophet had spoken hundreds of years before: "The Spirit of the Lord is upon me, because he has anointed me to proclaim good news to the poor. He has sent me to proclaim liberty to the captives and recovering of sight to the blind, to set at liberty those who are oppressed, to proclaim the year of the Lord's favor" (Luke 4:18–19 ESV).

Interestingly, "the year of the Lord's favor" is a reference to the biblical year of Jubilee, when all financial debts were forgiven. While Jesus is elevating this to mean that he is freeing us from our spiritual debts, it does not negate its original meaning. "It is for freedom that Christ has set us free" (Galatians 5:1). This is the way of Jesus. If we want to align ourselves with the heart of God, we must seek to free anyone, including ourselves, from the steel trap of credit predators.

Going Off-Trail

When I hike in the mountains, I always follow a very clear trail. Once, however, a sweet-smelling sage attracted me off the path. I stopped to breathe in the fragrance, then unwisely kept plodding away from the trail. After a few minutes of wandering from shrub to flower, I looked up and found myself face-to-face with a coyote the size of a well-fed German shepherd. Thankfully it only gave me a "wolf-nod" as it kept moving along.

When it comes to our financial lives, there is also a clearly marked *credit path* that we all need to stay on. This path is fairly simple: *Avoid borrowing from people who want to harm you.* Unfortunately, it is common to smell the sweet fragrance of "easy money" and wander off the credit trail by borrowing from credit predators who might harm us.

According to the Federal Reserve, 37% of Americans would be unable to come up with $400 without borrowing or selling something.[47] So we borrow—and we get devoured by interest. The most dangerous way we leave the credit path is by borrowing money from *payday lenders* or *credit card companies.* Consider the following recent statistics:

- 12 million Americans borrow using payday loans, and one in five cannot pay them back.[48]

- 56% of active credit card accounts have unpaid balances, averaging an eye-popping $7,279.[49]

Predatory Payday Loans

Payday lenders are clearly predators, charging 1,000% interest with the hope you'll need a new loan to pay for the old one. Their population has also increased to the point where there are now more payday lenders than McDonald's! As the British comedian John Oliver pointed out, "I didn't know there was more of *anything* in the US than McDonald's!"[50] Each year, 12 million borrowers take out payday loans, averaging eight loans of

$375 each and paying a total of $520 in interest.[51] Payday loans are advertised as short-term credit lines, typically extended for two weeks to help sustain consumers until their next paycheck. Most often they are used to cover essentials such as food, utilities, or rent.[52] But while $375 may seem like an insignificant loan amount, more than 80% of payday loans are rolled over within a month, so these small loans quickly turn into very big loans.[53]

For example, let's assume you take out a $200 loan over a fourteen-day period. If the payday lender charges $40, you may feel that's reasonable if it means you can pay your utility or grocery bill. However, when looking at the math, this situation easily can get out of hand. The $40 charge equates to a 20% *period* interest rate, or a 520% *annual* interest rate. Considering that most credit cards charge under 20% annually, this should cause you to pause.

However, the situation is much worse than we can imagine. Consider the earlier statistic that 80% of payday loans are rolled over within a month. This means that, for most payday borrowers, the interest of their prior loans becomes a part of their new loans (interest earning interest), which, unfortunately, grows exponentially. For your $200 loan, if you kept getting a new loan to cover your old loan, you would owe $22,900 after just one year! That equates to an 11,000%+ annual interest rate. While it may seem like I'm using hyperbole, it is actually true. Consider the tragic real-life example of Naya Burks. As a single mother living in St. Louis, her $1,000 loan quickly turned into $40,000 of debt.[54]

> Payday lending is a clear-cut example of *usury*, which means a lender is charging excess interest to a population that is financially vulnerable.

Modern-day payday lending is a clear-cut example of *usury*, which means a lender is charging excess interest to a population that is financially vulnerable. Usury has been universally condemned by every major religion and culture since the invention of banking.[55] Martin Luther, when witnessing this ensnarement of the poor, said, "Usury lives off the bodies of the poor."[56] The Bible consistently discourages charging interest among the financially vulnerable: "If you lend money to any of my people with you who is poor, you shall not be like a moneylender to him, and you shall not exact interest from him" (Exodus 22:25 esv). The Qur'an speaks to this issue in detail, saying that "those who devour usury shall not rise again…. God blots out usury" (2:275–80)[57] (the $4.2 trillion Islamic finance market is built around the prohibition of usury).[58]

Alternatives to Payday Loans

If you find yourself needing some cash *now* and are tempted by that payday lending store just down the street, consider one of the following less-harmful methods to get cash.

Best Alternative: Personal Emergency Fund

Having sufficient cash savings will eliminate almost all short-term cash crises. It allows you to provide an interest-free loan to yourself with no hard deadline for repayment. Everything works out great since you are very kind and generous to yourself! Simply multiply your run rate (see chapter 5) by the number of months you wish to save up for (three to six are most common).

Negotiation

Call your utility company or creditor to ask for extended payment terms. They are usually willing to work with you to avoid sending you to collections.

Pawn Loan

With a pawn loan, you offer something of value as collateral. If you can't pay the lender back, they simply keep the pawned item, and you owe nothing.

Credit Union Loan

Credit unions often work with consumers who have poor credit histories, allowing them to borrow up to $1,000 on a six-month loan at very low rates.

Credit Card

They are not ideal, but at least using a credit card means your interest rate will be 12–25% instead of 1,000%.

Employer Pay Advance

Some employers offer short-term loans to bridge the gap between now and your next paycheck.

401(k) or 403(b) Loans

It's possible to take out a loan from your employer-sponsored retirement account. The rates are lower than you can get anywhere else, but using this type of loan is rarely a good idea since you are invading money that is meant for the distant future, when you will likely be even more financially vulnerable than you are now.

Loan from Family or Friends

Receiving a loan from family or friends may or may not be a good idea. Consider it as a one-time-only option, and offer to pay interest (just not 1,000%!).

The Trojan Horse of Credit Cards

Credit card companies are actually craftier than payday lenders since they don't *appear* to be predators. A credit card company uses a hidden diabolical three-stage plan for devouring your finances: (1) dazzle, (2) hook, and (3) overpower and subdue. These stages parallel how the ancient Greeks offered the gift of a wooden horse to deceive the Trojans and secure their victory over the city.

Stage 1: Dazzle with Rewards

In the first stage, credit cards are portrayed as a way to buy things without needing to use cash. More than that, if we simply use our credit card instead of cash, we'll get cash back or free airline miles or free car rentals (etc.)! This first stage *dazzles* us with bright, exploding points that light up the night sky every time we swipe our cards. Most people who start using a credit card simply see it as a medium of exchange they will certainly pay off at the end of the month.

Stage 2: Hook with Dopamine

After we've been dazzled, we get *hooked* on using the Trojan horse and accept it into our home. Studies have shown that because credit cards allow us to delay the consequences of our spending, they remove a critical barrier to spending.[59] This is true even if we pay off our card each month. Put another way, credit cards trick our brains into spending more because we can delay paying until the end of the billing cycle. This sends a reward to our brain called dopamine, and the result is that we get a thrill from shopping.

Using cash is different. When I pay with cash, there is pain in every purchase. I hate counting out the money and handing it over to the cashier. I also hate getting coins back! If we shop using cash, we immediately experience the consequence of our shopping. For this reason, studies have shown that if you use cash for your purchases, you will spend 30% less.[60]

When I first saw this statistic, I didn't believe it would be true of me, so I decided to experiment with using only cash for my fast food purchases. I put $40 into a "Fast Food" envelope for the month, then went to Panera to buy a Mountain Dew. When the register displayed $2.80, it was the first time I noticed the price of my drink. I knew this was more expensive than a soda at Taco Bell, so I aborted the purchase, walked to the Taco Bell across the street, and spent $1.98 for my drink. In that moment, I confirmed the studies since I had just spent 30% less money!

Knowing this 30% statistic to be true for me, I have tried to go "all-cash" in the past, but the logistics of keeping cash in envelopes and carrying coins in our mostly cashless culture made it very difficult. Instead, my family uses digital envelopes to help contain our spending (see chapter 5). However, students have told me that when they were in a financial crisis, going all-cash helped them survive the storm.

Stage 3: Conquer with Minimum Payment

Having dazzled us with rewards and hooked us with the enjoyable feeling of dopamine, credit card companies employ the last stage of their plan by taking advantage of a flaw in the human brain known as *anchoring bias*. This means our brains anchor to information we see first. Credit card companies make sure we see a very attractive-looking number known as the minimum payment, knowing that we will anchor to it (e.g., $15). Once we do, it's too shocking for our brains to adjust to the larger full balance, so we naturally avoid thinking about it. The end result is that although most people never intend to use a credit card to borrow money, only 35% actually pay off their full balance.[61]

In the aftermath of repeated doses of dopamine, our minds become glazed over and less responsive. At this stage, we are anchored to a small payment and easily subdued as we are lulled into a "credit sleep." When we eventually wake up, we're unable to stop credit card companies from siphoning off our precious income for their benefit. In this way, they are like crafty beavers, building dams that become so entrenched in our lives that we can only helplessly watch as the income God has given *us* to manage is redirected toward *their* homes.

When we do not pay our balance at the end of the month, we have officially begun to borrow money from the credit card company. Although they offer a better alternative than payday loans, credit card companies are still horrible lenders, seeking to *conquer* us with high interest rates and lots of fees. If you pay only the minimum monthly payment of $76 on a $6,000 balance with an annual interest rate of 15%, it will take roughly 29 years to pay off your loan. In the end you will pay more than $20,000 of interest (remember how interest earning interest grows exponentially?).

Given these dangers, should you never use credit cards? I believe using them is a matter of common sense. If you find yourself borrowing from them, you should pay them off and then cut them up. On the other hand, if you are able to use credit cards to simply earn rewards and build a good credit score (see next chapter), then I think they have their place. Although the very nature of a credit card is to desensitize you from spending, a daily looking and tracking habit within the framework of a spending plan (chapters 4 and 5) should act as a sufficient guardrail to help contain this problem. Going all-cash is also a solution, but as I recently mentioned, this solution is one of the most difficult to pull off.

Debit cards are a good alternative to credit cards since they only act as a medium of exchange without the opportunity to borrow money.

One potential middle ground between digital and physical envelopes is where you combine a savings account, phone app, and debit card together under one service. The special debit card does not allow you to make purchases from your savings account until you designate what digital envelope will be used for any given expense (using the phone app). Qube

Money is one example of a company that is providing this type of hybrid money-tracking product.

My general rule is that I will cut up my credit card if I ever get to a place where I am charged interest or fees more than twice a year, indicating I am not responsible enough to use a credit card and am slipping into their trap. I would simply switch to using a debit card, which does not allow me to borrow money. Debit cards are a good alternative since they only act as a medium of exchange without the opportunity to borrow money. But be warned that they still slightly encourage spending since you "swipe and buy" without really seeing your money go away.

Selecting a Good Credit Card

By using a credit card, I enjoy getting hundreds of dollars in cash back every year. But I also use my card with much fear of what it can do to me, so I never let my guard down. As I just mentioned, I will immediately cut up my card if I ever find myself not paying off my balance at the end of the month.

If you are in a place where you can responsibly use a credit card, consider the following primary criteria for evaluating your choices. I personally do not care about a credit card's APR rate since I do not plan to borrow from the card *ever*. I also do not care about whether it has purchase protection since I can use my homeowners insurance to cover lost personal property (those who are not homeowners can purchase relatively cheap renters insurance that will cover personal property).

Favorable APR

Lower is better, but this doesn't matter if you're not going to use the card to borrow money.

Annual Fee

The better the rewards, the more likely you will pay an annual fee. In general, an annual fee is worth it only if the benefits will far exceed the fee.

Foreign Transaction Fee

It's much better to choose a card that will not charge this fee every time you use it outside the US.

Good Rewards

Usually it's a choice between cash back and travel points.

$0 Fraud Liability

Most cards have this feature; it ensures you won't have to pay any unauthorized charges.

Purchase Protection

This is short-term insurance protection from theft or damage on recently purchased items (usually within 90 days). It is a secondary coverage that will only apply if you do not have renters or homeowners insurance.

WHAT IF YOU'RE DENIED A CREDIT CARD?

- Ask a friend or family member to make you an *authorized user* on their credit card account. Of course, you would only make this request if you share mutual trust.
- If you are in school, try getting a *student credit card* from your parents' bank.
- Consider *credit-building credit cards* that are often easier to qualify for but have different measures for approval, such as a three-year banking history.
- Search online or ask your bank about a *secured credit card*, which allows you to put down a security deposit that can be returned after using your card responsibly for a certain period.
- If you are denied a secured card, try applying for a *credit-building loan* with a local credit union. You contribute regular amounts of cash that are eventually returned to you through a savings account. Once the loan is complete, the credit union will use the full savings account balance as a security deposit for a secured credit card.
- See *wholeheartfinances.com/appendix* (chapter 8) for suggested website resources.

WHOLE HEART EXERCISES

WHERE ARE YOU NOW?

When it comes to credit cards, I am ...

❑ Exposed. [Mark any statements that apply.]

» I pay late fees and interest charges on my credit cards.

» I don't really know how much things cost.

» It's hard for me to resist impulse-buying.

❑ Guarded. [Mark any statements that apply.]

» I never pay fees or interest charges on my credit cards.

» I discuss all big purchases with my loved ones before I buy.

» I use money I've already set aside for my purchases.

How guarded you are from the dangers of credit cards?

TOTALLY EXPOSED								HIGHLY GUARDED	
1	2	3	4	5	6	7	8	9	10

GUARD YOUR WHOLE HEART

Credit Cards

❑ Mark any statements that apply.

» I do not have a credit card.

» I have a credit card and have never paid fees or interest charges.

» I have a credit card and have paid a late-payment fee twice during the past twelve months.

» I have a credit card and have not paid a full balance during the past twelve months.

❏ If I marked either of the last two statements, I will stop using my credit card.

*If you are interested in shopping for a credit card, see the appendix for helpful websites.

Emergency Fund

❏ Calculate your ideal emergency-fund amount to cover expenses for three to six months.

CALCULATION	IDEAL EMERGENCY-FUND RANGE
[my monthly run rate [see chapter 5]] x 3 =	$_____
[my monthly run rate] x 6 =	$_____

❏ Mark any statements that apply.

» I have less than $400 of emergency funds to help me avoid future debt.

» I have at least $400 of emergency funds to help me avoid future debt.

» I have less than enough emergency cash to cover expenses for three to six months.

» I have emergency cash to cover expenses for at least three to six months.

❏ If you checked any boxes that include "less than," write down a plan to start building up your emergency fund.

_____

_____

_____

CHAPTER 9

THE 800 CLUB

A good name is to be more desired than great wealth;
favor is better than silver and gold.

PROVERBS 22:1 NASB

My younger brother, John, once competed to be recognized as the top symbol of school spirit among his graduating class. For the talent portion, John asked me to accompany him in a dramatized synchronized swimming routine. As we performed the comedic sketch, my mom and sister threw water at our nose-plugged faces as they hid behind a waterscape poster. It was such a big hit! In fact, after the competition, our reputation preceded us around town. For years my brother and I would get comments like "Aren't you those synchro guys?" and "I was laughing so hard I nearly spilled my coffee!"

Just as our synchro-swim reputation went ahead of John and I, a person's credit reputation also precedes them. And while Jesus did not entrust himself to people's thoughts and opinions (John 2:24–25), his disciples did stress that we should consider how our reputation precedes us:

Live such good lives among the pagans that, though they accuse you
of doing wrong, they may see your good deeds and glorify God on
the day he visits us.

1 PETER 2:12

[A church leader] must also have a good reputation with outsiders,
so that he will not fall into disgrace and into the devil's trap.

1 TIMOTHY 3:7

God calls us to be his vice-regents, which is basically another way of saying that he wants us to represent his interests on Earth. While it is okay for the world to hate us because of our love of Jesus, it is not okay for the world to hate us because we are dishonest or careless with money. Jesus said, "If you cannot be trusted with things that belong to someone else, who will give you things of your own?" (Luke 16:12 NCV).

Your Credit Report

In the world of finance, our credit reputation goes ahead of us whether we borrow money or not. At this moment, you may or may not have a *personal credit report*, which is created when you are involved in either obtaining credit to potentially borrow money or having a service extended to you before you pay for it (e.g., dentist, rental or utility service). It shows the world how trustworthy you have been when others have placed their trust in you to pay them back. Not having a personal credit report means you are *credit invisible*; you are like a stranger to every bank or landlord you try to do business with, which will often work against you.

> It is important that you become credit visible, because landlords and service providers want to know whether they can trust you to promptly pay them.

A credit report is about more than just borrowing money; it also shows whether you have paid your rent, medical, and utility bills on time. Any time you borrow money or set up an account where someone will wait for you to pay them, the business that is extending this type of credit will likely give your personal information to a credit bureau.

A credit bureau receives your personal information from creditors and compiles it into a credit report that anyone can access if they *pull your credit*. Landlords, employers, medical professionals, and lenders have the ability to do this if you give them permission. There are currently *three credit bureaus: Equifax, Experian, and TransUnion*. They started out serving specific geographical areas and eventually became nationwide services. While they each generate your credit report in a slightly different way, they should all have the same important credit information about you.

Everyone starts out as credit invisible to these bureaus. The most common way a person becomes *credit visible* is when they open an account to borrow money from a credit card company or student loan provider.[62] Even if you don't need to borrow money, it is important that you become credit visible by opening a credit card account or a utility account. This is important for two reasons: First, landlords and service providers want to know whether they can trust you to promptly pay them. If you have no credit report, they may make it difficult for you to be served. Second, when you establish a healthy record of being offered credit, and never using it, you build a solid foundation for getting the lowest-cost loan possible just in case you may need to borrow money in the future for a home or school tuition.

Steps to Excellent Credit

At a minimum, having a good credit reputation means that you pay your bills on time. However, if you stopped there, you would miss an important opportunity. The key step in having a credit reputation that precedes you everywhere you go is to build up your credit so that it is considered excellent. In the credit world, this refers to a credit score in the 800s, and those who achieve this are in *The 800 Club*.

Financial institutions often pay credit bureaus to determine a person's credit score using algorithms, with scores typically ranging from 500–800. The most popular score comes from the Fair Isaac Corporation, which generates a "FICO score" for anyone who is credit visible. If you have never borrowed money or opened a credit account, but are credit visible from renting an apartment or using a utility service, you will most likely maintain an average credit score in the mid-to-upper 600s. Having an 800 credit score, however, will show that you have a sophisticated understanding about how financial markets work. It also carries many additional perks:

- **Priority Housing:** When competition becomes fierce, landlords and sellers will often use a credit inquiry as a way to prioritize the queue. I have had multiple occasions when a landlord moved me to the front of the line after pulling my credit report. If you have average credit, you will likely stay in the middle of the line.

- **Cheaper Mortgages:** The difference in mortgage costs between an average and excellent credit score can be more than *$58,000 of interest* on a $400,000 loan.[63] The savings are significant!

- **Better Credit Card Rewards:** An excellent credit score will give you access to better rewards programs with credit cards, including more cash back, more airline miles, access to airport lounges, free online streaming services, cheaper concert tickets, and even free mugs and t-shirts.

Avocado trees are plentiful in my neighborhood, and given that grocery stores often charge more than a dollar for a single avocado, they may well represent the closest thing to money growing on trees! I was shocked when one day a new neighbor moved into a home with a well-established avocado tree and immediately cut it down. It was such a loss since that precious tree took decades to develop. Your *credit tree* is an investment that will provide services (shade) and benefits (fruit) throughout your entire life, even when you never have to actually borrow any money (cut your tree down for firewood). You must think about your credit as a tree that you plant, grow, and never cut down. Following are three steps that will help you become a member of The 800 Club.

Step 1: Establish a Long Credit History

The longer your credit history, the more likely your credit score will go up. If you are currently credit invisible, open a new credit card, use less than 8% of your available credit (see step 2), and pay off your full balance at the end of each month. This will start your credit-history clock. If you are being denied a credit card, see the steps in chapter 8 that detail how you can qualify. The easiest way is to become an authorized user on someone else's account.

Step 2: Gain Lots of Available Credit and Never Use It

Ensure that you are never using more than 8% of your available credit from credit cards while still paying your full balance at the end of the month. For example, if you have a card that provides $5,000 of credit each month, make sure you never use your card for more than $400 of purchases each month.

This is true even if you pay off your balance at the end of the month. *Credit utilization* is simply having a balance during the month, not having a $0 balance at the end of the month. If you are using more than 8% of your credit from credit cards, your credit score will not be excellent, but using between 10–30% will leave you in the range of a good 700 credit score. If you want to improve your credit utilization (i.e., use no more than 8% of your available credit), you will need to:

- Use your credit cards less (switch to cash or debit card).

- Sign up to pay your credit card twice a month. This will lower the overall amount of credit you're using.

- Ask your credit card companies to raise your credit limit (up to twice a year).

Step 3: Open Up New Credit Slowly

Ensure that you do not open more than one credit account at a time. Too many new credit inquiries will temporarily lower your credit score. Opening new credit or even having lenders process an application for new credit (i.e., a hard inquiry) will show up on your credit report in a way that lowers your credit score for a few months to a year.

In addition, when you increase your credit limit, as suggested in step 2, it's possible this can be viewed as an increase in new credit, so do not continually increase your credit limit if it is lowering your credit score (usually this happens for those with below-average credit scores). However, any harm that new credit does to your credit score is only temporary. If you are slowly growing your available credit over time and you never use it, your score will eventually soar.

Please note that these three steps apply only to managing credit cards. Other types of credit (mortgage, student and auto loans) impact credit scores differently than credit cards. While addressing how these loans impact your credit is beyond the scope of this book, a good guiding principle is to have a healthy fear of borrowing any money from any lender and seeking to repay any type of loan as soon as possible (more on this principle in the next chapter).

A Disturbing Crime

Unfortunately, it's possible to do everything right when it comes to credit—but still have a low credit score. The reason? Even if we stay on the credit path and establish a large credit line while using very little of it (i.e., low credit utilization), someone may steal our identity and trash our precious credit. This is called *identity theft*.

One of the most disturbing movies I have watched is *The Talented Mr. Ripley*, based on the 1955 novel by the same title. Tom Ripley grows jealous of his rich friend and eventually murders him and steals his identity. You would think the murder would be what disturbs me the most, but no. I am most disturbed when Tom Ripley parades around trying to consume his friend's former life.

My God-given identity is such a precious prize, so it is deeply disturbing to me when I witness identities being stolen. I have been the victim of identity theft two times. Both were minor situations, but they were still scary. When I was a sophomore in college, I opened a checking account and a few weeks later noticed three $40 charges for bounced checks. I had not written any checks recently, so I was confused. Later I discovered that someone had found a few "starter checks" I had thrown away in a dumpster after I received my permanent checks. It took me months to get the fees refunded. (This taught me early on that all important financial documents I discard should be shredded and not simply thrown away).

More recently, after a call from my employer asking if I had applied for unemployment benefits, I found out that my social security number had been stolen. Just like the first occurrence, I felt deeply violated when I realized someone was trying to steal my identity for their personal gain.

No Longer *If,* but *When*

It's said that the biggest question about identity theft is no longer *if* you will be a victim, but *when*. With 15 million victims every year,[64] identity theft is one of the fastest-growing crimes in America. During a recent three-year period, cybercrime complaints went up 71% (467,361 to 800,944), and losses from these complaints skyrocketed from $3.5 billion to $10.3 billion.[65]

TOP FIVE TYPES OF IDENTITY THEFT[66]

TYPE	NUMBER OF REPORTS	% OF TOTAL
1. Credit card (new accounts opened)	409,981	44%
2. Miscellaneous	263,419	28%
3. Bank fraud (new accounts)	110,513	12%
4. Tax fraud	78,588	8%
5. Business/personal loan	76,020	8%
Total	938,521	100%

While identity theft may seem like a problem among "grown-ups," many people don't realize that young children are common targets. Of the one million child identity theft incidents in a recent year, 50% involved children younger than age six.[67] If a child has a social security number, he or she is a potential victim.

A friend once told me that when she decided to check her credit as a college student, she thought she wouldn't even have a credit report (i.e., be credit invisible) since she had never used credit. To her surprise, she did have one—and it was more than thirty pages long! Someone had stolen her identity when she was ten; they had been opening up accounts and not paying bills in her name for many years. It took my friend more than three years to clear her report.

> Even if we stay on the credit path and establish a large credit line while using very little of it, someone may steal our identity and trash our precious credit.

Other common victims of identity theft are the elderly and the military. Of any age group, the elderly have lost the most. Members of the military are targeted because they're often deployed for long periods. Also, the more active you are on social media, the more likely you will become a victim. Users active on Instagram, Facebook, and Snapchat are at a 46% higher risk.[68] To manage these risks, let me encourage you to take one or both of the following important measures.

1. Monitor Your Credit Report

Regularly monitoring your credit report for activity you don't recognize is a solid first step. After accessing your free credit report online (see wholeheartfinances.com/appendix [chapter 9] for how to do this), make sure the information is correct, including addresses, credit accounts, credit inquiries, and records of repayments. If there is any activity you don't recognize, immediately spring to action to repair your report by working with the three credit bureaus (see the exercises for more details).

Currently you can look up your credit report for free up to once per week, but I recommend a frequency of once every six months. It is best to review all three reports at the same time. Each of the three credit bureaus should have essentially the same information, but occasionally one will feature unique information.

Often my students are hesitant to look up their credit report since they have been trained to never give out their social security number. This rule, while appropriate before the modern era of financial technology, is no longer viable. There are multiple documented examples where people's social security numbers were stolen from secure places like banks, credit bureaus, and the DMV. This means that our social security numbers are likely already "out there" even if we have never shared them with any consumer or financial website.

Personally, I pay an identity-theft insurance company $12 per month to actively monitor my credit reports by the minute. The service will let me know if there are any changes to my credit reports and will also help repair my credit if it's ever compromised. I could save money and do exactly what this insurance service provides, but I decided to pay the premium because they are saving me time and effort. I like knowing the very moment there has been a change on my credit report. I want to be as vigilant as possible in this highly deceptive world of deep fakes and catfishing.

2. Sign Up for Fraud Alerts

While it is very good to stop fraudulent activity soon after it occurs, it is even better to prevent it from happening. One easy (and free) way to do this is by adding a fraud alert to one of the credit bureaus (it will apply to all three bureaus). Once you add this alert, no new credit accounts can be opened until the credit bureau confirms with you that the credit inquiry is legitimate.

This fraud alert has worked brilliantly for me on many different occasions. Whether I was buying a phone, financing solar panels, or refinancing my mortgage, I had to clear each transaction with the credit bureau I set up the alert with before I was given any new credit. For example, when I selected a no-interest installment plan to pay for my new phone, the sales associate "ran my credit" by pulling my credit report (i.e., a hard credit inquiry). In the process, I was told I couldn't complete my purchase because there was a fraud alert in place on my credit. I then received a call from the credit bureau, asking whether this installment purchase was a non-fraudulent activity. I confirmed that it was and walked away with my phone.

Having a fraud alert on your credit is a powerful way to help ensure that no one will open up a credit account in your name. Take note, however, of a few important considerations. First, the fraud alert needs to be renewed every year. I have set up an annually recurring calendar reminder, and you may want to do the same. Second, having a fraud alert on your credit report *may* prevent you from being approved for a credit card. I've found that credit card companies will drop an application if they must jump through hoops because of a fraud alert. It is likely best to take the fraud alert off when you apply for new credit and then add it back after your account has been opened.

WHOLE HEART EXERCISES

WHERE ARE YOU NOW?

When it comes to credit, I am ...

❏ **Negligent.** [Mark any statements that apply.]

» I assume nothing will go wrong.

» I assume credit is not important for me.

» I see no visible threat to my credit.

❏ **Vigilant.** [Mark any statements that apply.]

» I actively monitor my credit for potential threats.

» I am watchful about changes to my credit.

» I patiently guard my credit.

How vigilant are you with credit?

NEGLIGENT									HIGHLY VIGILANT
1	2	3	4	5	6	7	8	9	10

GUARD YOUR CREDIT REPUTATION

See wholeheartfinances.com/appendix (chapter 9) to access useful website links when completing these exercises.

❑ Monitor your credit report.

» Download your free annual credit report from each of the three credit bureaus and ask the following questions.

1. Is all of the identifying information correct?

2. Is all of the credit account information correct?

3. Do you recognize every "hard inquiry" where a business has pulled your credit?

4. Have you filled out dispute forms with the credit bureaus and any applicable businesses?

❑ Make plans for future monitoring.

REQUEST ON THREE SEPARATE DATES		REQUEST ON A SINGLE DATE	
Date	**Bureau**	**Date**	**Bureaus**
	Equifax		Equifax, Experian, TransUnion
	Experian		
	TransUnion		

» Explore identity-theft insurance.

» Identity-theft insurance usually costs about $10–$20 per month and provides the following services:

• Credit report monitoring

• Real-time alerts whenever your credit report changes

• Repairs to your credit report if someone wrecks it.

❑ Add a fraud alert. A fraud alert means that if you or someone else tries to apply for credit in your name, the lending agency will first call and ask you for verbal verification that it is okay to open the credit account.

1. Call Equifax, Experian, or TransUnion to place a fraud alert on your account (a fraud alert at one bureau will apply to all three).

2. Add an annual renewal reminder to your calendar.

3. Remove the fraud alert if you're trying to open a new credit account. Otherwise, your application will likely be denied.

CHAPTER 10

A POUND OF DEBT

Debt is a great source of inner unhappiness.
ATTRIBUTED TO DEBASISH MRIDHA

I once lived with a roommate who confided in me that, after five years of working hard in his after-college career, his student debt only seemed to grow. I never had student loans, so I could only imagine how hard that would be.

Later that year, I received more money than I expected from an inheritance. As I was asking Jesus where this money should go, I got very excited about spending my surplus to help my roommate out of his debt. I told him my plans and watched as his shoulders slowly lowered from their tense position. Once he realized he was now debt-free, my friend almost collapsed in relief, as though an invisible boulder he'd been carrying on his back was now suddenly gone.

Jesus treats financial debt seriously because of how seriously it impacts us. He chose to compare the kingdom of heaven to a king who forgives financial debts (Matthew 18:21–35), and the apostle Paul also chose to use very explicit financial debt language in his letter to the Colossian church: "He made you alive together with Him, having forgiven us all our transgressions, having *canceled out the certificate of debt* consisting of decrees against us, which was hostile to us; and He has taken it out of the way, having nailed it to the cross" (2:13–14 NASB 1995).

In Shakespeare's play *The Merchant of Venice*, Antonio agrees to borrow money from Shylock (a Venetian moneylender). Like Romeo and Juliet, Antonio and Shylock come from backgrounds that have historically hated each other. Shylock devises a crafty plan to lend Antonio money without charging any interest. The catch is that if the original loan is not paid back, Shylock will cut a pound of flesh from Antonio.

What I dislike the most about this tragic tale is Antonio's carelessness. He knows the severe risk, and yet he agrees to the deal. Too often we do the same. Whenever a lender comes along to give us "free money," we echo Antonio's words: "Content, in faith. I'll seal to such a bond."[69] We then go about our day, not realizing we have voluntarily placed our feet securely in the steel trap of a hunter.

A Serious Affair

While financial debt is often hard to avoid, one thing is certain: We should always treat it very seriously. We've already discussed how at one time the word *mortgage* meant "death pledge." The language around debt and borrowing is severe for a reason. If you are in debt, you are said to be "in bondage." Within the corporate world, a common certificate that tracks the amount of debt a business owes is called a *debenture*, which is the same word for indentured servant, which refers to slavery for a period of time. This debenture certificate is also commonly called a "bond," like a Treasury bond, which comes from the word *bondage*.

In some ancient North African tribes, defaulting on credit was viewed as dishonesty that affected the entire community. The debtor could be sent away, cutting off his family relationships and protection from the tribe. Lenders in ancient India and Nepal were known to humiliate a borrower by sitting at his doorway and fasting until the debt was paid. If the lender died during the fast, villagers would beat the borrower to death.[70] In many ways, *The Merchant of Venice* is an allegory for how those who get into debt have the potential to lose a "pound of flesh" financially, emotionally, and spiritually.

Financial Loss

A debt contract often traps people into paying much more interest than they anticipated. During a recent three-year period, Americans paid about $120 billion in credit card interest and fees each year.[71] If you are charged

15% interest on a $6,000 credit card balance and make only the minimum monthly payment of $76, it will take you twenty-nine years to pay off your loan, including more than $20,000 of interest.

Emotional Loss

Research by Dr. Galen Buckwalter found that 23% of all adults and 36% of Millennials experience financial stress from debt at levels that would qualify as post-traumatic stress disorder.[72] One study found that higher debt was associated with worse physical health,[73] and another study associated it with worse mental health.[74]

Spiritual Loss

The Bible frequently warns that having debt means you have invited another master into your life who may diminish your understanding of your freedom in Christ. Proverbs 22:7 says, "The rich rule over the poor, and the borrower is slave to the lender," and Romans 13:8 advises, "Owe no one anything, except to love each other, for the one who loves another has fulfilled the law" (ESV).

After the Israelites fled Egypt, God gave them the Sabbath as a reminder they were now free people (only free people can take a day off from work!). However, when free Christians choose to work without rest, it is not long before they forget they are free. In the same way, when we take on financial debt, we become beholden to another. If we get behind on payments and experience the psychological trauma of constant calls from collectors, or making choices between food and credit card payments, it is harder to express our freedom in Christ.

Is Debt Immoral?

Because of the dangers just discussed, it is easy to conclude that debt is immoral, but this is not true. First, let me disclose to you that I currently have debt—a mortgage that helped me purchase my home and a loan that helped me purchase solar panels for my roof. You may conclude that whatever I am going to say, I'm simply trying to justify my "financial sin." That will be for you to decide.

Jesus almost seemed to celebrate the idea of lending when he had the primary protagonist of one of his parables say to a wicked steward, "You should have put my money on deposit with the bankers, so that when I returned I would have received it back with interest" (Matthew 25:27). Bankers are able to pay interest to depositors because they are lending money and charging interest to others. At the very heart of lending is a simple service where people with extra money and few good ideas are putting their money to work by giving it to people who have no money and lots of great ideas. To ban lending would seriously inhibit the financing and development of new businesses and services.

However, while lending is likely not inherently immoral, there is a *type* of lending that is immoral, as we've already discussed. Someone who lends to the poor and charges an excessive interest rate (i.e., usury) will eventually "own" that vulnerable person, and for that reason, usury is completely immoral.

In the end, a Christian's decision to accept or reject debt is mostly a matter of wisdom, not morality. Wisdom implies the correct application of knowledge. And with debt, there is a key pearl of knowledge that every Christian must learn how to apply: distinguishing between two distinct types of debt.

Two Types of Debt

Debt on *depreciating assets* is like stepping into quicksand. The only wise thing to do is escape and never go near it again. Debt on *appreciating assets* is mostly neutral in effect, but it does have the potential to be very harmful under certain circumstances. This type of debt is like walking on a rickety bridge to cross a deep ravine—it may serve a valuable purpose, but be very, very careful!

1. Depreciating Assets: Caught in Quicksand

In financial terms, the word *depreciate* means the value of something goes down over time. Depreciating assets deteriorate from use and eventually need to be replaced. They include cars, computers, clothing, furniture, and appliances. This type of debt is truly unwise for two reasons. First, you must make a triple payment to get out of it (see chapter 6). This is usually very difficult to do. Second, there is usually very little reason to need debt in the first place because vibrant used markets already exist where you can buy these assets cheaply. With a little proactive planning, you can pay cash for what you need and at a fraction of the cost for new.

I made a decision to always pay cash for my cars, knowing if I were to lease or make a car payment, I would lock myself into a cycle of debt with that triple payment. After buying my first vehicle, Sandpiper, for $2,000 at auction, I saved up another four years for my next car—a used Hyundai Accent, which I paid cash for. Five years later, I had enough saved for a slightly nicer used Toyota Prius V.

> To ban lending would seriously inhibit the financing and development of new businesses and services.

As our family drives our current car, we are always saving for our next car. We save about $180 every month in a virtual envelope called "New Car," which grows in value over time. We've driven over 120,000 miles in our Prius (named Blue Steele) and hope to continue to save for another four years. Then we plan to pay cash for a nice, used minivan.

In general, simple math dictates that debt on depreciating assets should be avoided at all times. Don't allow debt beavers to build a debt dam that will actively siphon off a significant portion of precious income that God has given you to steward.

2. Appreciating Assets: Crossing a Precarious Bridge

Borrowing for an *appreciating* asset is different because the loan is backed by a type of asset that, in most cases, goes up in value over time. This is an important distinction. Typically, this growth will more than pay for the cost of the interest of the loan, so in general the lender does not gain power over the borrower.

In the case of a home, the growth of its price over a long period of time often will be many times greater than the interest cost. School loans may work this way too. When you borrow to pay for a bachelor's degree, the interest expense is matched against the growth of your salary. Most studies show that the return on investment (ROI) of a college degree is both positive and significant. One report showed that over the course of their careers, those holding a bachelor's degree earn on average $1.2 million more than those with only a high school diploma.[75]

Borrowing to buy an appreciating asset should be considered less dangerous than borrowing to buy a depreciating asset. However, you must have a reasonable expectation that what you are buying will appreciate over time. Those who buy a home at peak prices or take out school loans with plans for low-earning careers (e.g., a youth pastor or painter) will end up with debt on a non-appreciating asset.

TWO TYPES OF DEBT

1. DEPRECIATING ASSETS	2. APPRECIATING ASSETS
• Value goes down over time	• Usually increase in value
• Like getting caught in quicksand	• Like crossing a rickety bridge
• Always avoid if possible	• Can be helpful, but be very careful

Our Response to Debt: Four Strategies

If we ever do end up in a situation where we are considering debt, the first step of wisdom is to fear it. A particular scene from the literary classic *O Pioneers!* has replayed in my mind many times. Siblings Lou and Alexandra are talking about Alexandra's plan to increase their acreage in the hopes they'll eventually become independent farmers.

> **Alexandra:** "The next thing to do is to take out two loans on our half-sections, and buy Peter Crow's place."

> **Lou:** "Mortgage the homestead again? ... I won't slave to pay off another mortgage. I'll never do it. You'd just as soon kill us all, Alexandra, to carry out some scheme!"

I love Lou's response. He is angered at the idea of getting back into debt. We should never acquire debt without first reckoning the complete financial, emotional, and spiritual cost. And if we do end up taking out loans, we should seek to explode our debt dams by aggressively paying them back.

Paying back debt is a relatively simple process for those who have just one loan. If you have more than one, however, there are a few different repayment strategies that you can adopt. Financial experts have largely used a mountain motif to illustrate four approaches (Avalanche, Snowball, Bear Vault, and Switchback), so I will continue with that tradition.

As I explain these different repayment strategies, let's assume you have two debts: (1) $10,000 of school loans with an annual interest rate of 8.5%, and (2) $750 of debt from purchasing furniture at a 5.5% annual interest rate.

1. Avalanche (high interest first)

Debt with the highest interest rate is paid off first, so in our example, the school loan would be paid off before the furniture. This strategy will always result in the least amount of interest paid. It is the quickest way to get down the mountain (i.e., an avalanche).

2. Snowball (low balance first)

The lowest balance is paid first, so you would first tackle the furniture debt of $750. Even though this may not be mathematically efficient, behaviorally it may cause you to gain enough momentum (snowball effect) to pay off both loans since you will feel so elated by getting rid of one of your debts. Paying off debt in this way can be more motivating since you often get to experience success early on.

3. Bear Vault (consumer loans first)

This strategy does not look at interest rates or balances but seeks to pay off *consumer debt* (i.e., depreciating assets) first. Like a bear that raids your camp on a regular basis, debt on depreciating assets causes you to get into more debt to replace assets as they wear down. Getting rid of consumer debt first (in our example, the furniture) essentially puts your precious living essentials into a "bear vault" so the credit-bear menace can no longer steal your essentials each night. This strategy is both highly efficient and motivating.

4. Switchback (consolidation)

This strategy would seek out a new lender to give you $10,750 to pay off both the school loan and the furniture loan at once. By consolidating, you move from having multiple lenders to just one. This strategy is great for a person who is disorganized. It also has the potential of lowering overall interest costs, but there are many factors to consider. Quite often you end up paying more overall interest. Be careful when considering consolidating school loans since some of the flexible repayment options may be lost.

DEBT REPAYMENT STRATEGIES

STRATEGY	1. AVALANCHE	2. SNOWBALL	3. BEAR VAULT	4. SWITCHBACK
Description	• Pay off high interest debt first	• Pay off the lowest balance first	• Pay off depreciating consumer debt first	• Consolidate debt and pay off one loan
Advantages	• Least amount of interest • Quickest	• Motivation from early success	• Efficient and motivating	• Efficient • Sometimes results in lower interest

WHOLE HEART EXERCISES

WHERE ARE YOU NOW?

When it comes to debt, I am ...

☐ Casual. [Mark any statements that apply.]

» Debt is no big deal.

» I don't know how much debt I have.

» I don't know when I will pay off debt.

☐ Fearful. [Mark any statements that apply.]

» I'm scared of debt.

» I create a repayment plan the moment I even consider debt.

» I look at all other options before considering debt.

How fearful are you of debt?

IT'S NO BIG DEAL									I'M TERRIFIED
1	2	3	4	5	6	7	8	9	10

COUNT THE COST

See wholeheartfinances.com/appendix (chapter 10) to access useful instructions and website links when completing these exercises.

☐ Calculate how much debt you have.

1. Access your free credit report to determine how much non-government debt you have.

2. Access the amount you owe on any government-funded school loans.

DEBT I OWE

LENDER/ SERVICER NAME	LOAN TYPE	AMOUNT	INTEREST RATE	GRACE PERIOD	ESTIMATED MONTHLY PAYMENT

Monthly Total: $_____

❏ If you have more than one type of debt, determine a repayment strategy.

» Avalanche

» Snowball

» Bear Vault

» Switchback

❏ Write down the details of your debt repayment plan.

1. My next monthly payment: $_____

2. Year I expect to be debt-free: _____

3. Restaurant, event, or other reward to celebrate being debt-free:

_____

4. The person who will hold me accountable to sticking to my repayment plan:

_____

PART 4

SAVE WITH YOUR WHOLE HEART

Growing Your Giving through Saving and Investing

It is vanity to be concerned with the present only
and not to make provision for things to come.

THOMAS À KEMPIS, *THE IMITATION OF CHRIST*

CHAPTER 11

BANK AS BASE CAMP

Suppose a woman has ten silver coins and loses one.
Doesn't she light a lamp, sweep the house
and search carefully until she finds it?

LUKE 15:8

Fresh off our wedding, I walked into our little apartment one morning and told my wife, "Honey, I'm so sorry, but I accidentally married you to the sea." She was confused until I showed her my bare ring finger. A look of sadness swept over her face as she realized that my custom-engraved gold wedding ring had fallen into the sea during a surfing session. Although I have since replaced it, I still return to that surf spot, peering into the water like Gollum, searching for "my precious" ring among the salty water and sand.

It is disarming to realize just how vulnerable our precious possessions are to loss, theft, and misplacement. During Jesus's teaching ministry, he instructed his followers, "Do not store up for yourselves treasures on earth, where moths and vermin destroy, and where thieves break in and steal. But store up for yourselves treasures in heaven, where moths and vermin do not destroy, and where thieves do not break in and steal. For where your treasure is, there your heart will be also" (Matthew 6:19–21).

Ultimately, we are not meant to treasure material things of value. While I love my wedding ring, it is a temporary, material thing. It is better to treasure what is permanent. Given just how precious and permanent Jesus is, treasure him and let stuff just be stuff; it is given to us for a time to help achieve the good purposes of God.

As we strive to do this, however, where do we put valuable possessions like cash, jewelry, or bond certificates? While we are not meant to treasure them, surely we need to put them somewhere. During Jesus's day, people's homes were the only places where things of value could be stored, making them vulnerable to theft and misplacement. Consider the opening line to one of Jesus's parables: "Suppose a woman has ten silver coins and loses one" (Luke 15:8).

Wait! Stop right there. Although this parable of the lost coin is about God's intense love for us, I can't help but notice how stressful it would be to have all your wealth sitting around your house. While I cannot say it is unbiblical to keep money in your personal residence—where fire or thieves can destroy at any moment—I can say that keeping money in a bank is a much less stressful way to store things of value. However, banks are not places that are entirely without danger, which this chapter will address.

Bank on It

I once came across an Instagram post from an Airbnb host who was complaining that one of her guests stole her cash. She was paranoid that a bank would take her money, so she kept several hundred dollars in a mason jar. Ironically, the more this woman tried to avoid loss from a *bank*, the more exposed her money became to loss. This is similar to someone who is so worried about crashing their car that they crash their car out of worry about crashing their car.

A few years after the pandemic, the nation of Lebanon experienced an economic and social breakdown. The banks had stopped giving people their money back, so ordinary citizens showed up with guns and "robbed the bank" to get their own money back. This is a nightmare situation that no one wants to have happen in the US.

Yet the probability that the US dollar will completely implode, ushering us into an apocalyptic financial world, is very low. The US dollar is the world's reserve currency, and no country or digital currency is in a position to change that anytime soon. A collapse of the US banking system has never occurred, although the US banking system was less stable prior to the creation of the

FDIC (Federal Deposit Insurance Corporation). Now, almost every bank deposit is FDIC insured, which means that even if a sophisticated ring of robbers breaks in and takes your money, the US Treasury Department will refund you up to $250,000 per bank.[76]

On the flip side, the probability of experiencing loss while keeping money outside of a bank is dramatically high. A common occurrence (at least in our family) is misplacing valuables—for example, loose cash and jewelry. It's especially easy for items such as these to get lost in a move. Consider also that during a recent year, close to fifteen million homes were destroyed by natural disasters, including wildfires, hurricanes, blizzards, and tornadoes.[77]

On a more sinister note, a US home is burglarized every fifteen seconds (2.5 million annually).[78] And when it comes to home theft, a common robber, unfortunately, is family. There are countless stories where family members have stolen from their loved ones in desperation. Tragically, over a quarter of child identity thefts are perpetrated by friends and family.[79] Given these types of statistics, I would be very wary of storing valuables outside of a bank.

The probability of experiencing loss while keeping money outside of a bank is high.

My home has been robbed before (not by family, thankfully). One beautiful spring morning, we left at 9 a.m. for an appointment, and when we came back at noon, the house was a mess. Since we had two toddlers, it took a few moments before Tammy and I realized something was amiss. We were shocked that a hostile stranger had been in our home. The police officer who investigated remarked, "This kind of thing never happens here"—and yet it did.

For cash kept at home, most insurance companies will reimburse you no more than $200 to cover a robbery or fire—much less than the FDIC's $250,000! And once your money is in a bank account, you will not misplace it in your jacket or under your car seat (I'm looking at you, Sage and Silas!). The bottom line is that the risk of losing money at a US bank is much lower than the risk of fires, floods, theft, and misplacement.

Gateway Checking Accounts

Apart from a bank offering a more secure place to put your money, it is also a critical cultural gateway for your financial life. All your spending, giving, and saving efforts run through your bank "base camp" to work out the calling the Lord has given you. Without a bank account, you lose access to many critical modern services.

For example, paying bills in today's economy is very difficult (nearly impossible) to do with cash. Most service providers want to be paid with a check, a credit card, or an *Automatic Clearing House (ACH)* transaction.[80] Banks offer ACH transactions as a service that allows you to "wire" money without any fees. It is often a great way to pay, especially if you have a credit card but want to protect your credit score by using it less (i.e., having a lower utilization). Having a bank account will also give you access to investment services (e.g., buying stocks and bonds), charitable giving services (e.g., sending money to your church), and tax services (e.g., getting a tax refund much faster).

If you are ever denied a basic checking account, you can collect the cash and coins stored away in your house and mimic a checking account's services by purchasing a prepaid debit card from a convenience store or any number of vendors. This prepaid card can then be used to pay bills online and store your crumpled up cash and coins. While this allows you to pay bills without having a bank account, your money is uninsured by the FDIC and highly exposed to loss or theft. Also, these cards do not improve or build your credit and may include monthly fees.

The Bank Bank-Robber

Besides the unlikely implosion of the US banking system, another reason people sometimes object to having a bank account (i.e., being banked) is that banks, themselves, are robbers. If this is what you think, you are not wrong!

Consider Stan's all-too-common story. At age eighteen, he opened his first checking account with his life savings of $950. He was excited about his new financial freedom. He signed up for overdraft protection since that sounded like a great idea, and he used his debit card for most purchases. After a few months, however, Stan checked his balance and noticed a barrage of fees. He couldn't quite understand what was going on. He tried to build up cash to cover any overspending, but the fees just kept coming and depleted his savings. Stan decided he would not use a bank anymore and keep his earnings hidden in his room.

While this may not be your story, it is a repeated story among the financially vulnerable. Bank fees are often confusing and predatory by nature. US consumers paid $17 billion in overdraft (paying the bank to move money from your savings to your checking) and non-sufficient funds (NSF) fees (paying the bank a fee for not having enough money to cover a transaction) in a single year, which amounts to $53 for every American.[81]

Ironically, customers who sign up for overdraft "protection" often suffer the most from overdraft fees, which are largely avoidable by simply saying no to this service when it's offered by a banking representative. Every time an account holder accidentally does not have enough money to pay a bill that is drawing from their checking balance, overdraft protection automatically draws the needed funds from the customer's savings account.

Behaviorally, however, it is much better to have more separation between your checking and savings accounts so you don't treat your savings like a cookie jar you can easily draw from. One solution is to open a savings account at an online savings bank, which will also likely generate 60–80 times more interest than a savings account at a commercial bank (more details later in this chapter).

In addition to overdraft fees, commercial banks often charge ATM fees, monthly service fees, paper-statement fees, foreign-transaction fees, and account-closure fees. Checking fees are completely avoidable, but more than one in four Americans are paying monthly fees that average $24, or $288 per year.[82] I do not pay any checking account fees, and neither should you. In general, to avoid fees, adhere to the following tips:

- Avoid signing up for overdraft protection so you can create a healthy barrier between your savings and checking accounts and earn much more interest with a separate online savings account.
- Arrange for your paychecks to be automatically deposited.
- Use only ATMs that are included in your bank's network.

If you find that your bank is actively trying to take advantage of you with fees, it is probably time to find a new bank. When looking for a new bank, be sure to consider credit unions. But how is a credit union different from a bank?

Credit Unions: Act like You Own the Place

The moment you open an account with a *credit union*, you do not have to "act" like you own the place—you actually own the place. Every account holder is part owner. This is different from private banks, who are owned by shareholders. As an account holder at a credit union, you have a vote in what fees are charged and what products are offered. Each year you will receive voting materials and the chance to attend membership meetings.

Credit union products and services are essentially the same as commercial banks, but with better customer service and lower fees.

Credit unions may also have a unique tax-favored status that allows them to charge less than commercial banks for products and services. This status is only available if the credit union requires a certain type of "field membership" for their account holders, meaning it is exclusive to a certain type of group. Typical field memberships include professional groups (e.g., military, K–12 teachers, trade unions, medical community), locales (e.g., Southern California, Dallas), and community groups (e.g., school alumni, rotary clubs, church denominations).

Credit union products and services are essentially the same as commercial banks, but with better customer service and lower fees. Deposits are insured up to $250,000 from the National Credit Union Share Insurance Fund (NCUSIF), which is considered as strong as the FDIC. Credit unions with the most exclusive, unique qualifications (e.g., military, work-related groups) often have the best deals and services, but they also may have the least amount of branch accessibility.

The biggest strength of a commercial bank is better accessibility and potentially lower fees for ATMs or safe-deposit box access. I use a commercial bank simply because I live right next to one and rent one of their safety deposit boxes. If at any point they disrespected my business or charged fees I could not avoid, I would instantly switch to either a teacher credit union (my sister is a K–12 teacher, and credit unions are usually open to family members) or my alma mater credit union (fight on USC Trojans!).

Online Savings: Low-Hanging Fruit

Banks can also become bank robbers by not providing any interest. In this way, they are robbing you of what you should be getting. To illustrate, let me use one of my favorite stories: *Pride and Prejudice*, by Jane Austen. My favorite scene of Darcy and Elizabeth getting together still gives me chills:

> **Darcy:** "If your feelings are still what they were last April, tell me so at once. *My* affections and wishes are unchanged."[83]

My second-favorite scene is actually much less romantic. It involves annuity and interest rate calculations. *Swoon!*

> **Elizabeth:** "For five thousand a year, it would not matter if he's [Mr. Bingley] got warts and a leer."[84]

Knowing that Mr. Bingley received $5,000 a year and that banks typically provided 5% interest at that time allows me to calculate all sorts of estimations about the wealth of Mr. Bingley and the net worth of the aristocracy during that period. My wife just rolls her eyes when I geek out on discovering the financial situation of Jane Austen's characters.

When looking at our financial situations, we should all roll our eyes when banks give us 0% interest rates on our savings accounts. For hundreds of years, banks have traditionally provided 4–5% annual interest,[85] but today, commercial banks will give you mostly nothing for savings accounts. It is a new cultural development that interest rates during the last thirty years are the lowest they have been over a five-thousand-year period.[86]

A low interest rate, in many ways, is a "hidden tax" on savers. The *Wall Street Journal* calculated that savers missed out on $42 billion in interest in just one quarter because they kept their money in commercial-bank savings accounts.[87] Just about every time I walk into my bank, they try to persuade me to open a savings account and are shocked when I say no. I then express my shock that their savings accounts provide so little interest.

Thankfully, as previously mentioned, there is a very easy way to earn 60–80 times more interest than what commercial banks are currently offering: Simply open an account with an *online savings bank*. These banks are often well-established physical banks in a different country or a type of financial institution that does not provide traditional banking services (i.e., a credit card company).

Because online savings banks provide purely online banking services, they save a lot of money by having no physical branches. Their savings are then passed on to customers in the form of higher interest rates. The only drawback is that transfers to your checking account can take one to two days. This could cause a cash flow crunch if you need to pay a bill right away. This has happened to me only once during the last twenty years—I was short $100 for paying a bill, so I asked a friend to instantly transfer cash to my account via a phone app. I paid a $1 charge and reimbursed my friend the next day.

A typical online savings account is FDIC insured up to $250,000, so you can earn 60–80 times more interest with no additional risk. This is truly "low-hanging fruit" for you and your household.

WHOLE HEART EXERCISES

WHERE ARE YOU NOW?

When it comes to storing my money, I am ...

❏ Unbanked. [Mark any statements that apply.]

> » I am always worried about theft, fire, and misplacement.

> » I lose out on earning interest.

> » I have no access to modern day services and products (many people don't even accept cash anymore!)

❏ Banked. [Mark any statements that apply.]

> » I know banked money is much safer than unbanked money.

> » I like that I am insured up to $250,000.

> » I have access to modern services and products.

Which number best indicates how much of your financial life is banked?

ALL CASH AT HOME								FULLY BANKED	
1	2	3	4	5	6	7	8	9	10

GET BANKED

See wholeheartfinances.com/appendix (chapter 11) to access useful instructions and website links when completing these exercises.

❏ Evaluate your checking account. [Continued on next page.]

» Questions to ask:

1. How much money is required to open an account? What is the minimum balance?

2. What fees are possible with this account? How can I avoid them?

3. When are deposits available for me to use? Are reloadable debit cards available? What are the fees?

» If you do not have an account, you will need the following items to open one:

1. Pick 2: state-issued ID, passport, social security card, birth certificate

2. Social Security Number (SSN) or Individual Tax Identification Number (ITIN) (if you don't have an ITIN, consider applying for it online)

3. Proof of physical address, such as a utility bill

4. Initial deposit

» If you are denied a checking account:

1. Order a ChexSystems, Early Warning, or TeleCheck Service report. Pay outstanding balances. If there is a mistake, fill out a dispute form.

2. Shop for prepaid debit cards. Load money onto these cards and use them to pay bills and receive paychecks.

3. Consider using a credit union.

❏ Open an account at an online savings bank, link it to your checking account, and transfer money from your checking account into your new savings account. Be aware:

» The online savings bank with the highest interest rate usually offers this rate only for a few months (i.e., a teaser rate).

» While transfers between your online savings account and checking account are free, they may take one to two days to settle. Try to keep enough money in your checking to weather regular expenses.

CHAPTER 12

GATHERING AN ELDER-YEARS RESERVOIR

Lift up thine eyes to the good things of heaven,
and thou shalt see that all these worldly things are nothing,
they are utterly uncertain, yea, they are wearisome,
because they are never possessed without care and fear.
The happiness of man lieth not in the abundance of temporal
things but a moderate portion sufficeth him.

THOMAS À KEMPIS, *THE IMITATION OF CHRIST*

When I was thirteen, I was filled with angst. It wasn't uncommon for me to swear at my friends or steal a candy bar from the local convenience store. Like many teenagers, I did not quite know what to do with all my hormones, and I also made very bad choices. However, one good choice I made was to attend my church's incredibly fun and welcoming youth group. Each summer we went to Hume Lake Christian Camp, and I slowly began to take steps toward loving Jesus.

A few weeks after my first summer camp session, I was home alone and decided to write a letter to a girl I had met there (yes, we sent physical letters back then). As I went outside to mail the letter, I accidentally locked myself out of the house. But I quickly came up with a brilliant plan to climb a tree next to the house, jump onto our balcony, and enter the house through the unlocked screen door. Everything went perfectly—except the part where I fell two stories onto a rod iron fence.

I can still feel the wind rushing past my ears as I fell. It's a miracle I am still alive. When I woke up after the sixteen-hour surgery to remove a spike from my body, the surgeon told me he was so proud I was alive that he wanted to keep the spike. I politely said no.

I lay in my hospital bed for many weeks, a seventy-pound bag of bones. I had nothing to offer anyone, and I was completely helpless and poor. Yet I never felt wealthier, because I could sense that Jesus was present in my room. I don't know how to explain it except that I felt his smile and was assured that he truly knew me and accepted me. It was incredible. This relationship was a priceless treasure placed into my tiny, bony hands.

Jesus's love and personal attention made me the richest man alive. It was a taste of heaven that I can still taste to this day. Nothing else compares. Now that I am in my forties, this experience has made saving for retirement different for me than for many others. I would never call my retirement savings a true treasure. For me, having God's love is like having the brightness of the sun, while having a storehouse of money for retirement is like having a flickering candlestick.

In one of his parables, Jesus accuses a farmer of being a fool because he thought his retirement savings were his true riches. Jesus described a fool as anyone who "stores up things for themselves but is not rich toward God" (Luke 12:21). "Rich toward God" can also be translated as "rich in relationship with God." If I were to rephrase this verse, I would add, "A fool is someone who does not see their relationship with God as their true riches, but instead pours all their devotion and affection onto their worldly treasures."

As we grow old, our health and ability to earn income are compromised. This is a reality that we all must address since it will impact our ability to care for ourselves and others. Even though more than a quarter of Americans have no money saved for their elder years,[88] most of us understand that we will likely live beyond our ability to earn income and that building a storehouse of money, or *elder-years reservoir*, is a very important endeavor.

However, it is a grave mistake to blindly build wealth. There is a balance to be found between the dangers of wealth and the reality that an elder-years reservoir can be a powerful tool for our lives of generosity. Not finding that balance will likely make us both spiritual and fiscal fools.

Seashells and Sunsets

When you see or hear the word *retirement,* what is the first image that comes to mind? Whenever I ask students or adults this question, they consistently say gray hair, golfing, sailboats, seashells, sunsets, and sandy footprints. But what if I told you these images have nothing to do with the original concept of retirement?

In 1828, Noah Webster's *An American Dictionary* listed one of the definitions of *retirement* as "the act of withdrawing from company or from public notice or station."[89] But today, one of Webster's definitions is "withdrawn from one's position or occupation: having concluded one's working or professional career."[90] This change in definition is tragic!

A recent study found that those who have longer working lives also have longer life spans with higher well-being.[91] Another study found that people who delayed their retirement by one year increased their longevity by 11%.[92] Put another way, the earlier you stop working, the quicker you die.

> There is nothing better for a person than that he should eat and drink and find enjoyment in his toil. This also, I saw, is from the hand of God.
>
> Ecclesiastes 2:24 ESV

This idea of work being essential to our general well-being is evident in the story of Adam and Eve. After God created them, he immediately put them to work. He didn't say, "Go ahead and work until you're older, and once you've put in your dues and have suffered long enough, I will release you from your heavy burden and allow you to live out your remaining days as one big vacation." Instead, he designed them to work, play, and rest simultaneously.

When I was working at a large investment firm near the beach, I and a few other employees would come in an hour early so we could take a two-hour surf break each day. My boss would often see me in the afternoons with my hair wet and my shoulders relaxed, the salty smell of the sea still on my lips. One day he said, "I bet you're excited about the day when you can retire and stay at the beach all day, every day." My response was not what he was expecting: "That sounds horrible. Too much beach spoils the enjoyment of the beach. My dream is to do what I am doing now: working and surfing together."

Work is more meaningful when combined with rest and recreation. And rest and recreation are more meaningful when combined with work. Often, when people are desperate to retire, they are simply burned-out and need to find a way to have more rest in the rhythms of their working life. While it may sometimes seem like work is "bad" since it is under a curse because of Adam's sin (Genesis 3:17–18), our endeavor to work has always been good since we are literally "made to do it." And in Christ, the curse is being redeemed. Timothy Keller explains,

> When we work, we are ... the "fingers of God," the agents of his providential love for others. This understanding elevates the purpose of work from making a living to loving our neighbor.... Work not only cares for creation, but also directs and structures it.... The purpose of work is to create a culture that honors God and enables people to thrive.[93]

Preserving Your Ability to Be Generous

Despite these truths, the reality is that there may come a time when we are physically unable to work and generate earned income. Because this period can be decades long, it is also a worthwhile endeavor to have an elder-years reservoir—a pool of income we can draw from to help sustain ourselves and our ability to be generous.

For thousands of years, the elder-years reservoir of most cultures has been children taking care of their parents. In a Christian setting, if this was not possible, the church should have stepped in (1 Timothy 5). In today's culture, while the church may still step in for special situations, the historical approach of managing your elder years is largely not accessible because children do not expect to take care of their parents. Cultural anthropologists Ellen and Lowell Holmes write,

> At every point in the American life cycle, evidence points to a lack of family solidarity, cooperation, or reciprocity. With this kind of

ethos, societal members can expect little support in old age either from families or from an independence-oriented society.[94]

In America today, a "nest egg" (retirement savings) is most likely the surrogate family that will take care of us in our elder years. This new solution is not morally bad, but I do think there is a great loss to mourn when we are no longer expected to reciprocate within the family unit. Paul's vision for Christians was that those who are strong (i.e., income-rich) would take care of those who are weak (i.e., income-poor):

> I do not mean that others should be eased and you burdened, but that as a matter of fairness your abundance at the present time should supply their need, so that their abundance may supply your need, that there may be fairness. As it is written, "Whoever gathered much had nothing left over, and whoever gathered little had no lack."
>
> 2 CORINTHIANS 8:13–15 ESV

The current paradigm of retirement savings prescribes that we use an elder-years reservoir to ensure that we never have to be helped (i.e., we are never weak). Western culture's outrage at financial dependence is reflected in sentiments such as this:

> There are few things in life more important than independence—the knowledge that you can take care of yourself.... Creating a reality in which you are financially independent allows you to take care of yourself while planning for the future. Knowing that you can take care of yourself offers a healthy dose of pride.[95]

Despite the tragic loss of vibrant, interdependent communities who manage the income-poor years of our elderly, there are still positive merits to the American way of using savings to maintain strong elder years. A household who sustains their consumption independent of others requires much less coordinating and probably has less conflict and more overall choices available to them.

Avoiding the Perils of Wealth

While saving for our elder years may be necessary, it is not without peril to our material and spiritual lives. The following three steps can help ensure that you build your elder-years reservoir in a wise way: (1) connect to your future self, (2) recognize the eighth wonder of the world, and (3) surrender your reservoir daily.

Step 1: As you save, connect to your future self.

The first thing to remember is that you are saving for your future self. Have you ever thought about your future self? What does he/she look like? Will he/she be more mature? In what way? If you have never considered the needs of your future self, you are not alone. Even though it's inevitable that many of us will not have earned income in the future and our children will likely not be able to take care of us, our society is still not saving. Consider the following statistics:

- One out of every four Americans has no retirement savings.
- 49% of people ages 55 to 66 had no personal retirement savings (that's half!).[96]
- The US retirement-savings deficit was recently estimated to be $3.68 trillion.[97]

Future Self-Continuity (FSC) is an area of research that has become popular as policymakers and academics have tried to understand why people are not saving for their elder years. If you don't feel connected to yourself in the future, you lack future self-continuity. Academics often try to understand why people tend to place less importance on future rewards when compared to current rewards. They easily dismiss any activity that has a current cost, even if it has a big future reward (e.g., retirement savings). One study found that "to those estranged from their future selves, saving is like a choice between spending money today or giving it to a stranger years from now."[98]

As you can see, before you even begin the process of thinking about saving for your future self, it is important to get connected to your future self. As a Christian, you have an incredible future self who is becoming more like

Christ every day: "We all, who with unveiled faces contemplate the Lord's glory, are being transformed into his image with ever-increasing glory, which comes from the Lord, who is the Spirit" (2 Corinthians 3:18).

However, your future self is also becoming more and more vulnerable physically, which creates a financial vulnerability. As a Christian, we understand this tension: "Though our outer self is wasting away, our inner self is being renewed day by day" (2 Corinthians 4:16 ESV). We can decide today to enrich our future inner self by abiding in Jesus, picking up our cross and following him. We can enrich our future frail outer self today by making preparations for our season of no earned income, praying that God might teach us to "number our days that we may get a heart of wisdom" (Psalm 90:12 ESV). In both cases, we express a key fruit of the Spirit—self-control—as we take steps to bless our whole future self, who is both physical and spiritual.

Step 2: As you save, recognize the eighth wonder of the world.

We can't say for sure that Albert Einstein once called compounding interest "the eighth wonder of the world,"[99] but there is no question that this wonder is the reason I pursued a career in finance. As a young teenager, I was captivated by the idea that interest could earn interest. It created in me a sense of awe and wonder. If you are not immediately awed by this amazing invention, then you probably do not understand how it works.

Compounding interest involves a deposit of money that is able to generate a return (i.e., interest) over time. If the account continues to earn a return, then the previous return will also now earn a return (i.e. interest earning interest). While this may not seem like a life-changing event, consider that anything compounding on itself grows exponentially.

Exponential growth is one of the most powerful forces found in nature. Exponential growth of cells is what allows for human life; exponential growth of pathogens explains how one infected person can rapidly cause a worldwide shutdown; and exponential growth of faith in Christ explains how Jesus's twelve disciples turned the whole world upside down.

If you simply deposit money into an account that earns a rate of return, you harness this exponential power that looks like a hockey stick: At the beginning, the growth is not that impressive. But give it just a little time, and things go vertical. Compounding interest is really the only reason our modern idea of "saving for retirement" is possible.

Consider the following illustration. Assume you want to have $700,000 for your elder-years reservoir when you turn seventy in twenty-five years. If you store your money in your pillowcase, you would need to average saving $2,333 every month. If instead you take advantage of monthly compounded interest by generating a 10% return on your savings (usually by investing in the stock market; see the next chapter for more details)—and having *that* return generate a return—you can get away with *saving 77% less* ($528 per month). If you start just five years earlier, you can save only $310 per month (41% less per month by simply having five more years of time).

Compounding interest is really the only reason our modern idea of "saving for retirement" is possible.

Harnessing this greatest invention makes any type of savings plan much more attainable. And by saving a little bit longer, your required savings amount drops significantly. This is one reason why financial planning is so useful—you give yourself more time to achieve what God has placed on your heart, which almost always requires money.

Step 3: As you save, surrender your reservoir daily.

Our elder-years reservoir is like a crown that must be continually laid at the feet of Jesus (Revelation 4:10). We must always be looking for opportunities to both give and save. We must live in a way where we plan to take advantage of exponential growth, but also remain available for unscripted generosity that may create an adventure story we treasure for all time.

Bill and Vonette Bright, who founded Cru, one of the largest evangelical organizations in the world, are a beautiful example of this. Shortly before his death, Bill shared his story with the Generous Giving organization. Rather than taking his retirement money when he reached that age, Bill gave the full amount to launch a church-leadership training school in Russia. Many years later, Bill got sick and required expensive medical treatment. He had no money for it, but close friends introduced him to a Russian doctor who felt led to treat him for free. Despite not having his retirement fund, God used Bill's investment to take care of him in a beautiful way.[100]

Bill Bright's story may not be your retirement story. For the majority of people, God uses an elder-years reservoir as a part of his provision during your retirement years. I would challenge you, however, to stay open to winds that may blow suddenly, calling you to an untamed flow of giving that is "not of this world" (John 18:36).

WHOLE HEART EXERCISES

WHERE ARE YOU NOW?

When I think about my future self, I feel ...

☐ Disconnected. [Mark any statements that apply.]

> » My future self is a complete stranger to me.

> » I rarely think about doing things today that would bless my future self.

> » I do not seek to cultivate a bounty of self-control in my life (one of the fruits of the Spirit).

☐ Connected. [Mark any statements that apply.]

> » My future self is highly connected to my current identity. I often think about my future self and get excited about becoming more like Jesus Christ.

> » I seek to take steps today that will ripple into the future in a positive way.

> » I seek to cultivate a bounty of self-control in my life (one of the fruits of the Spirit).

How connected to your future self are you?

TOTAL STRANGER									BEST FRIEND
1	2	3	4	5	6	7	8	9	10

BUILD AN ELDER-YEARS RESERVOIR

See wholeheartfinances.com/appendix (chapter 12) to access useful instructions and website links when completing these exercises.

❏ Connect to your future self.

1. Download an aging app and generate a picture of your future self.

2. Imagine your future self going through a typical day of work and rest. Imagine that you are more like Christ since he promises that the Holy Spirit will continually transform you into his image (2 Corinthians 3:18).

3. Write down two things you can do today to help your future self flourish during your elder years.

❏ Determine your monthly savings for an elder-years reservoir.

» Choose simple calculation #1 (save 10% of your annual income throughout your life) OR simple calculation #2:

1. Determine the annual income you want to receive during retirement (in today's dollars): $_____

2. Multiply the amount above by 15 to determine how much you should have saved when you want to stop earning income: $_____
(15 times your income allows for compounding interest to buoy your savings while you draw from it during your elder years)

» Appendix retirement calculators

1. Enter the income you desire to have during retirement.

2. Make sure you adjust the optional inputs.

3. Be prayerful about every assumption.

❏ Surrender your elder-years reservoir to Jesus.

1. Read Mark 14:1–11. The cost to Mary of Bethany was great, but her reward was spectacular. Wherever the gospel has been preached, Mary's story has been told.

2. As you plan to build your elder-years reservoir, commit yourself to the Lord and allow him full sovereignty over your future self. Recognize that he is good and wants to use your investment planning to showcase his provision.

CHAPTER 13

INVESTING YOUR RESERVOIR

[The King] sent for the servants to whom he had given the money,
in order to find out what they had gained with it.

LUKE 19:15

One of my favorite passages in the Bible is the story of Gideon (Judges 6). It begins with Gideon threshing wheat in a winepress. This is a strange place to be threshing since it is located in a narrow hole below the ground where there was no wind and likely not enough room to get the job done. Wheat needed to be threshed on a large stone above the ground, where the wind could separate the chaff. But Gideon was afraid of the oppressive Midianites, so he wanted to hide his wheat harvest in an unlikely location.

Many of us end up with our investment money wasting away in a winepress. Whether it's because we fear hostile forces who want to take our precious resources or we have just been too busy to pay attention, often our elder-years savings ends up buried in a pillowcase or a commercial-bank savings account that earns 0.01% interest (i.e., a winepress).

Practically speaking, it is not ideal for long-term savings to be buried in a small hole where it serves no useful service. In the parable of the talents, Jesus illustrates kingdom truth by talking about the pitfalls of a servant who buried his master's money in the ground (Matthew 25:14–30; Luke 19:11–27).

God has designed communities to thrive as we take our savings and put them to work on community threshing floors. The purpose of this chapter is to explore the traditional, time-tested ways to earn a solid rate of return. In chapter 14, we'll explore the redemptive nature of our long-term savings invested over our lifetime.

The Benefits of Barbeque Sauce

I love barbeque. For me, the meat is just a canvas for the sauce. If the meat is dripping, spicy, and slightly tangy, I am a happy man. Many years ago, my immigrant friend shared with me his special homemade barbeque sauce. When I first tasted it, my eyes brightened and I smacked my lips.

"This is amazing!" I said. My friend gave a humble nod in reply, then turned his head and gave a far-off look. "This sauce is my passion. I want to sell it, but I have not been able to raise money to build my business."

Give this man some capital! I thought. After praying about it, I decided to provide an investment that would help launch his company. I hoped to benefit my community in three ways:

1. We could enjoy better food together.
2. My friend would gain meaningful employment.
3. A business would be created that would likely earn a fair rate of return for investors.

This trifecta of benefits for the community is how investing is supposed to work. It is a positive feedback loop: As God invests in us, we invest in each other. We receive money from God and then prayerfully spend, give, save, and invest it. As we do this, we indirectly generate more products and services that directly generate more income, ideas, and capital. It is a wonderful cycle of innovation and provision.

What kills this loop is when people either exaggerate far-off dangers or passively do nothing, which in both cases keeps money stuck in a personal account (i.e., winepress) that earns little to no return and helps no one. Once savers stay indoors and hole away money in a cash account, investment into the community comes to a halt.

Earning a Strong Rate of Return

The majority of Americans have no foundational knowledge about investing. As mentioned earlier, only about 35% of Americans are financially literate. Another study found that only 24% of Millennials understood basic financial topics.[101] As a culture, we are generally ignorant about how investing works.

A few years ago, comedian Will Ferrell poked fun at this lack of investing knowledge in a comedy sketch. He is digging through the floor of a studio stage, covered in dirt, when one of his friends walks up and asks what's going on. Their conversation goes something like this:

> **Will:** "I buried treasure here many years ago, and now I need it."
>
> **Friend:** "Great! How much?"
>
> *Will grabs an envelope with some cash and begins counting it.*
>
> **Will:** "Five hundred … huh?"
>
> **Friend:** "Oh, no! You buried only $500?"
>
> **Will:** "Back in 1995, I invested my $500—I should have at least three times that by now."
>
> **Friend:** "Oh … That's not how investing works."
>
> *Long pause.*
>
> **Will:** "I am very upset right now."[102]

When we begin the process of saving for an elder-years reservoir, many of us, out of fear or simply ignorance, "bury" our money somewhere in an effort to ensure that we do not lose it. The most likely place we bury our money is in a savings account earning close to 0% interest.

In Jesus's parable of the ten servants, one reason the master was so upset with the third servant was because he actually ensured a loss by burying it. "You wicked servant!" the master said. "Why didn't you deposit my money in the bank? At least I could have gotten some interest on it" (Luke 19:22–23 NLT).

Although it seems counterintuitive, if you try to avoid loss by putting your money somewhere safe, you actually guarantee a loss for yourself. This loss is experienced in two possible ways:

1. The loss of *purchasing power* from inflation, meaning the value of your original investment shrinks every year.

2. The loss from *opportunity cost* as you miss out on what you could have earned with that buried money.

The stock market, over long periods of time, has been an incredible creator of wealth, generating on average an 8–12% return per year. This means that everyone has a high opportunity cost when they bury their money. Even if you don't want to risk losing money in the stock market, or your financial needs are short-term in nature, making the stock market inappropriate, an online savings account would earn you 60–80 times more interest than a savings account at a typical commercial bank—without additional risk (see chapter 11).

When we put our elder-years savings in a place that earns little to no return, we lose. When we invest in a way that earns a healthy rate of return over a long period of time, we harness the power of compounding interest, which grows our savings exponentially (see chapter 12).

This, then, enables cheaper access to financing for the creation of products and services. It is a win-win for the investor and the business community since long-term investing (more than ten years) is a much safer way to manage money than burying it. Often when people refuse to expose their money to reasonable risk, they are acting more like the sluggard from Proverbs 22:13, who, instead of going outside in order to productively serve the community, justifies not working by saying, "There's a lion outside! I'll be killed in the public square!"

But how does "investing in the stock market" actually work? It is a long, twisty road, involving a lot of people and intimidating terminology. Here is a graphic for the process, and each part will be explained.

The Greatest Invention

Whenever I've asked my students to name the greatest invention over the last two hundred years, the most common answers have included cell phones, antibiotics, computers, and the internet. I'm still waiting for the day when someone will reply, "The Limited Liability Corporation."

As Ron Harris, a professor of legal history, explains, "Notable contemporary observers, including the Presidents of Columbia and Harvard, viewed the *Limited Liability Corporation (LLC)* as the greatest single discovery of modern times, surpassing steam and electricity."[103] What is not commonly known is that the LLC has been the primary catalyst for just about every modern invention during the last two hundred years, including cell phones, antibiotics, computers, and the internet.

Inventions require money, and the LLC supercharges a business's ability to raise funds by allowing it to form its own separate entity: the corporation. Once a corporation is a separate entity from its investors, it takes on full legal liability, allowing investors to buy fractional shares of ownership with limited legal risk. The most these *shareholders* in a corporation can lose is the money they put into it. Prior to the LLC, opportunities to invest in businesses were scarce, and if you did happen to score a partnership in a business venture, you were exposed to potential losses that were greater than your initial investment.

With as little as $1, any individual can invest in incredibly new and exciting products and services, such as electric cars, cancer medications, and artificial intelligence technology. The LLC has also enabled businesses with good ideas to receive millions of dollars to push them to market quickly. While these benefits have helped society innovate, they have also come at a cost. These *agency costs* and other dark sides of the LLC will be explored more in the next chapter.

Traders and Brokers

Investing in shares of stock has been shown to generate a healthy rate of return over the last 150 years. On average, you should expect to make between 8–12% per year when buying a stock collection of major US corporations. Since 1929, there have been only four instances when the average of all major US stocks declined two or more years in a row (only once, during the Great Depression, did it decline four years in a row). Buying a broad collection of stocks is a time-tested way to take advantage of the power of exponential growth.

So how do you buy shares of stock? The short answer is that you use a broker's app or website to open an account, transfer money from your checking account, and enter an order for the broker to buy stock for you. The broker will do so at a market where people are buying and selling those shares of stock. Stock markets are found in every major city around the world and are filled with traders (i.e., market makers or specialists) who act like matchmakers, helping buyers find sellers.

On average, you should expect to make between 8-12% per year when buying a stock collection of major US corporations.

Brokers have licenses that allow them to perform this service. Brokers connect with the traders in a stock market and make a trade on your behalf. In today's world, brokers electronically send buy orders to traders, who use sophisticated order books that automatically match buy orders with sell orders. The moment a buy order from a broker is matched with a sell order from another broker, a trade happens, and the agreed-upon price between the two parties becomes the last trade price of the stock.

Brokers and traders both charge for their services. Brokers charge a *commission*, and traders charge the *bid-ask spread*. For example, if you opened an account with a broker and placed an order to buy one share of Home Depot, the broker would find the *stock market* where Home Depot has traders actively matching buyers and sellers. For most major US corporations, this is the New York Stock Exchange (NYSE).

This broker would deliver your order to the trader of Home Depot at the NYSE, and the trader of Home Depot would match your order with a different broker who represents a client with a sell order of Home Depot. Your broker would then negotiate a price on your behalf using the instructions you gave them (most people buy at the current *market price*; i.e., a *market order*).

If your broker is successful, a trade will occur, and you will officially own a share of Home Depot stock. The broker will charge a commission fee, and the trader will have already charged you through the bid-ask spread fee (i.e., the buyer being forced to buy at the higher ask price and the seller being forced to sell at the lower bid price, and the trader pocketing the difference).

Both of these fees have come down dramatically over time as technology has allowed this entire transaction to happen in seconds through the use of computers and trading algorithms. When I was a teenager, the broker would charge a 9/16th commission on any trade involving less than 100 shares. This meant if I gave my broker $100 to make a trade, I would be charged a $56 commission! Thankfully, it is much better now. Because of advances in technology, most brokers charge a $0 commission for their services. Most orders to brokers are simple enough that the broker automatically routes your order to an in-house computer-platform tool that completes their service for you within seconds. The bid-ask spread (trading fee) will always be charged for every trade, but it can be as little as a penny for popular stocks.

The Mutual Fund Advantage

After opening an account with a broker, your first step is to transfer money from your checking account to your broker account. Once the money is with your broker, you can place an order to buy shares of a corporation. But what shares should you buy?

Entire industries and college majors are devoted to training people how to pick stocks that will generate a high rate of return. I studied stock valuation for decades, and it was not uncommon to spend four weeks (40-plus hours per week) researching one corporation before generating a report on its worth. During this time, I had access to the CFO, top industry intel, and seasoned investment veterans.

Your situation is likely different. You probably don't have the time or desire to dedicate yourself to the art and science of researching stocks. If I were to tell you to do this, you might feel the same way I would about changing the oil in my car: "Gross. I'd rather pay someone else to do that."

If this describes your reaction, you are in luck! A great product called a *mutual fund* was invented around 1924, and it allows investors to pay someone else to do the painstaking research and pick stocks for them. The fee they charge is called the *expense ratio*, which is a percentage that the mutual fund company subtracts from your account every year (expense ratios can range from 0.02% per year to 2% per year).

First, the company sponsoring the mutual fund product creates a pool of money (i.e., *fund*) sourced from lots of people (i.e., *mutual*). Next, this pool of money is handed over to a portfolio manager who does the stock research for you. Portfolio managers tend to specialize in certain types of stocks. The name of the mutual fund product will often broadcast what type of stocks the portfolio manager is buying. For example, the portfolio manager for a "small-cap US utilities fund" is buying only stocks in US utility corporations that are small in size.

Mutual Fund Products

Mutual fund products are many and varied. They can be classified by *size* (micro, small, mid, large), *industry* (e.g., health care, technology), or *style* (growth, value, blended). *Style* refers to the portfolio manager's investment philosophy: A *growth* manager focuses on relatively young corporations that are growing their sales rapidly. A *value* manager focuses on corporations that are out of favor by the average investor. The goal is to find stocks that have strong profits but are priced low since investors are uncertain about the prospects for those businesses. Growth versus value is an investment "philosophy" since people tend to naturally gravitate toward either way of thinking.

Exchange Traded Funds (ETFs)

If you want to buy shares in a mutual fund, you could open an account with a mutual fund, send them money from your checking account, and place an order to buy shares in their pool of stocks. This way is fine, but there are a few landmines to navigate. Traditional mutual funds have multiple share classes that may charge excessive fees (e.g., A, B, or C shares). There are also high minimum investment amounts for the classes that have lower fees (e.g., I shares).

One way around this problem is to buy a mutual fund product using an *Exchange Traded Fund (ETF)* option. ETFs are mutual fund shares that you buy in the same way you buy shares of stock. They were invented in the 1990s to help mutual fund companies more effectively buy all the stocks they needed for their products.

Instead of in-house staff ordering thousands of shares of stocks from their brokers, an ETF company is able to simply give a *buy list* to a professional *authorized participant*, who will use sophisticated technology and trading capacity to buy and package the buy-list corporations as one *ETF share*. This mutual fund product then issues shares of their product on a stock market (usually NYSE's Arca market), and customers can simply buy their product through a broker, like a stock.

Index Funds

How do you go about picking a good mutual fund product? In general, of course, it is good if they charge low fees and generate higher returns than their competitor products. However, the vast majority of them (75–90%, depending on what study you reference) consistently earn rates of return that are lower than the overall stock market.

Instead of randomly trying to find a product that will perform better than the overall stock market, you can "buy the market" by choosing a mutual fund product that is an *index fund*. This type of fund buys all the stocks available in the stock market and is called *passive* or *index* investing. It became popular in the late 1990s–2000s with the creation of the S&P 500 index mutual fund product, which buys all the stocks on a list of top-500 US corporations, generated by a financial rating company called S&P Global Ratings. Currently the most popular mutual fund product in the world is Vanguard's passive index product, the Total Stock Market Index Fund. This product gives any investor the ability to buy most major stocks from around the world with only a 0.02% cost per year.

MUTUAL FUND PRODUCTS

CLASSIFICATION	DESCRIPTION
Size	Micro, Small, Mid, Large
Industry	Health Care, Technology, etc.
Style	Growth, Value, Blended

Just because passive index products tend to outperform active portfolio managers does not mean that active portfolio managers are wasting their time. Up to 25% of active managers consistently outperform the computers. I was part of an investment company that outperformed the index for decades. Once I transitioned into teaching full-time, I didn't think I would be able to keep up with discerning the right managers or the right stocks, so now I mostly invest in a "passive way," primarily through "buying the market" with index products. I do this because I like the lower fees and the probability that I will outperform most other professionals (but not all). However, I do not simply buy the most popular index product in the marketplace. First, I need to pay attention to how any index product I own would impact society. This idea will be discussed in the next chapter.

Earn a Tax-Advantaged Rate of Return

Whether you are working with a broker to buy stocks or buying a mutual fund product to do the work for you, you will typically have a choice of whether to open a taxable or tax-advantaged account. If you are saving for your elder years, you most certainly want to open a tax-advantaged account since these accounts are made for just that (they are often called retirement accounts).

Every time one of your stocks or mutual funds generates a gain or dividend income, you are likely going to have to pay taxes on it. However, there is a beautiful way to minimize this tax. Because there is a crisis in retirement savings, the US government has created certain types of savings accounts that are sheltered from taxes (i.e., tax-advantaged accounts). The two primary ones available today are a *401(k) retirement account* and an *Individual Retirement Account (IRA)*.

A 401(k) account is available only if your employer provides access through their sponsorship. If this is the case, you should likely prioritize this type of investing account over any other since most employers are required to "match" into your 401(k), which means they would double any contribution you put into the account (usually up to 3% of your salary).

An IRA, however, is available to everyone who is working, regardless of whether their employer sponsors it. If you are under age eighteen, you can open an IRA through a custodial account. You can also open a Roth IRA, which tends to be favorable over the traditional IRA because you do not have to pay taxes on withdrawals you make once you reach age 59½.

If you are investing for your elder years, you will want to shield the exponential growth of your investment from taxes. This can easily happen if you save in either a 401(k) or an IRA tax-advantaged account. Allowing your elder years reservoir to grow tax-free means you will bend the exponential curve and see it grow even faster. However, please be aware that under most circumstances, there are penalties if you withdraw money from these accounts prior to age 59½ (although this age and other retirement-account rules are subject to change). One of the primary advantages of a taxable account over a tax-advantaged account is that withdrawals are allowed prior to age 59 without any penalties.

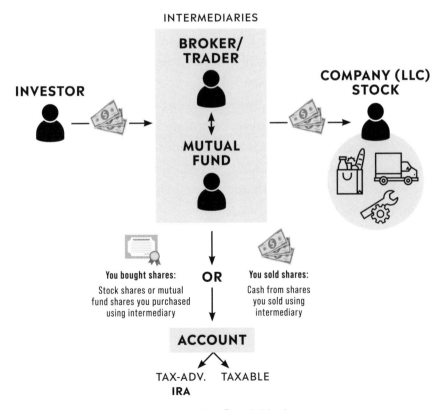

Investing in the Stock Market

The Virtue of Boring

As you invest, you may hear whispers or loud shouts from your friends about easily gained riches. Ignore this siren song! When we put God's money to work to earn a healthy rate of return, we should be focused on using his money to buy assets that provide useful products and services for society. It is a slow process that will lead to great gains over a long period of time because of compounding interest. This also aligns with the wisdom of Proverbs 13:11: "Wealth gained hastily will dwindle, but whoever gathers little by little will increase it" (ESV).

Avoid financial shortcuts, because chasing after get-rich-quick schemes is often just veiled greed.

Thousands and thousands of boring investors have simply bought and held a boring portfolio of stocks, which grow exponentially over time. There are also thousands and thousands who chased after quick riches and went bankrupt both financially and emotionally. In fact, this road to destruction is so well-worn that the Bible clearly warns against it: "Watch out! Be on your guard against all kinds of greed; life does not consist in an abundance of possessions" (Luke 12:15).

Avoid financial shortcuts, because chasing after get-rich-quick schemes is often just veiled greed. Instead, we are meant to be content with what we have been given: "Godliness with contentment is great gain.... For the love of money is a root of all kinds of evil. Some people, eager for money, have wandered from the faith and pierced themselves with many griefs" (1 Timothy 6:6, 10).

WHOLE HEART EXERCISES

WHERE ARE YOU NOW?

When it comes to long-term savings, my money is ...

☐ Buried. [Mark any statements that apply.]

» All of my long-term savings is in cash, losing value due to inflation.

» I have been burned by the stock market in the past, and I will never trust it again.

» I would not be able to handle seeing my money fluctuate in value.

☐ Multiplying. [Mark any statements that apply.]

» My money is given to businesses who are providing a reasonable rate of return over a long period of time.

» I am looking to grow my long-term savings exponentially over a long period of time.

» I will not panic if my money loses value because of a temporary market recession.

What is the status of your long-term savings?

BURIED									MULTIPLYING
1	2	3	4	5	6	7	8	9	10

MULTIPLY YOUR MONEY

For the following exercises, see wholeheartfinances.com/appendix (chapter 13) for helpful websites and further details on how to complete these exercises.

❑ Open a Roth IRA and research the stock and mutual fund options available to you.

» A Roth IRA is available to anyone over age eighteen.

» You can contribute up to $6,000 a year as long as you have earned income.

» Once you contribute, consider the money gone until you are at least 59½.

» After that, you can reap the rewards of tax-free exponential growth that will help you accomplish the goals God has placed on your heart.

❑ Take full advantage of free money by contributing up to the match limit in your 401(k) or other employer-sponsored account. It is hard to find a better return for God's money than employers who double your contribution up to a certain amount.

❑ Decide which areas of investing you will handle on your own and which parts you will outsource to a financial professional.

CHAPTER 14

THE REDEMPTIVE POWER OF YOUR RESERVOIR

We as a wise son or the wise daughter seek to avoid these schemes of bad profit in favor of the opportunities for good profit.

FINNY KURUVILLA

As I prepared for my first job interview at age fifteen, I was extremely nervous. My parents, through their sage coaching, helped me calm down and took me shopping for nice clothes that would impress the Taco Bell manager. I came home feeling empowered to face my interview with a slick, blue-collared shirt and a nice pair of khakis. When my parents helped me in this way, they literally "invested" in me. You see, the word *invest* comes from the Latin word *investire*, which means "to clothe"[104] (in-*vest*-ment; think of a vest that is often worn under a jacket).

Jason Myhre of Eventide Asset Management explains that this definition is found many times in the Bible.[105] In the garden of Eden, after Adam and Eve tragically betrayed God by eating the forbidden fruit, God "invested" in them when he covered them with animal skins (Genesis 3:21). In a much more spectacular display of God's love, we are said to be clothed with Christ (Galatians 3:27), meaning that God generously invested in us by clothing us with the righteousness of his beloved Son. And right before Jesus ascended to heaven, he told his disciples to stay in Jerusalem until they had been "clothed with power from on high" through the Holy Spirit (Luke 24:49).

In today's culture, however, the word *invest* doesn't evoke images of clothing or garments. For the most part, we think of the stock market where people in suits give money to big corporations in order to earn a return. While this may seem very different from the original definition, it actually is not. Investors are still investing in the traditional sense, except instead of covering businesses with clothing, they are covering them with money (capital) so they can produce a product or service for the benefit (or detriment) of our society.

The Dark Side of the Limited Liability Corporation

As Christians, are we doing a good job of clothing businesses with capital in a way that serves a redemptive purpose? At this point, you may have decided that "buying the market" is the best option for investing your elder-years reservoir (i.e., retirement fund), meaning you would invest in a mutual fund that buys a broad basket of stocks, like the S&P 500 index.

This option is attractive since it has the lowest cost of any mutual fund product, and you will beat most professional money managers (up to 90% of them!). However, before you go out and purchase this type of product, you must also consider how owning stocks may impact both your integrity and our world.

The Limited Liability Corporation, with all its benefits, has enabled shareholders to become less connected to the business they own.

There is a certain pride in owning and profiting from corporations that are making great products (e.g., good food) and providing essential services (e.g., hospital care). But what if one or more of these businesses are acting in a way that violates an investor's moral convictions? For example, someone might feel strongly that it is wrong to slaughter cattle for meat consumption, then discover they're partially funding their retirement with profits from McDonald's. The investor's integrity would be compromised if he or she did nothing.

Integrity is defined as "the quality or state of being complete or undivided."[106] *Integrity* comes from the word *integer*, as in "whole number." When a person loses integrity, their heart becomes fractured; they are no longer whole. One of the main psychological consequences of losing integrity is the gradual erosion of one's sense of self.[107] Many investors today are at risk of losing their integrity because they're profiting from behaviors they believe to be morally wrong.

The Limited Liability Corporation, with all its benefits, has enabled shareholders—the true owners—to be more at risk of losing their integrity as they are less connected to the business they own. This is the dark side of the LLC. While it was a marvel to allow a corporation to become a separate legal entity, it also drove a wedge between the managers and the actual owners. These managers are called *agents* since they are meant to represent the interests of the owners (shareholders).

However, this does not always happen. *Agency cost* is a well-documented phenomenon where agents of a corporation act in ways that are not in the best interest of the owners. A classic example of this would be a CEO who decides to use the company jet for family vacations (i.e., the agent is using company property in a way that is contrary to what the owners of the property would want).

The potential for agency cost has increased exponentially over the past several decades with the explosion of mutual funds and index investing.[108] Investors who purchase shares in funds that include hundreds of corporations usually do not know what they own. Christian stock owners, who have clear biblical guidance about good standards and ethical practices that make the world flourish, often may not know they own businesses that are exploiting labor and the earth for short-term profit, or funding abortion clinics, pornographic products, or other harmful products or services. For one of the most popular investment products, it has been estimated that 50% of its 500 corporations are acting directly against biblical values.[109]

PetroChina Thought Experiment

Assume you are making an investment decision in the year 2001. You buy a popular mutual fund that gives you exposure to stocks around the world at a low cost, and with a potentially good long-term rate of return. For some random reason, you decide to look up the list of all the stocks you now own as a shareholder. You see unsurprising names such as Apple, Starbucks, and Walmart, but one name stands out: PetroChina.

As you begin to research PetroChina's business model, you find out they pay a large fee for the right to drill oil in various countries, then sell the oil to the highest bidder. Along the way, you discover that PetroChina pays the Islamic Sudanese government large sums of money to drill, and Sudan in turn uses that money to cleanse the country of South-Sudanese Christians, using their hired assassins, the Janjaweed.

After buying your world index product, you are now faced with an ethical question: Is it morally acceptable that you now own a few shares in PetroChina? Does your ownership entail any type of ethical responsibility? Put another way, are you enabling the actions of PetroChina and the Sudanese government by owning shares?

Whenever I lead my students through this thought experiment, I receive three types of responses. Some immediately want to sell the index product since they don't want to potentially profit from a business that is helping finance a genocide. Other students immediately defend their stock position, arguing that a "secondary shareholder" is not causing any of the actions of the firm. Lastly, some students are simply apathetic.

During the first year of the Russian invasion of Ukraine, I changed the country for my students from Sudan to Ukraine and was not surprised to find that any apathy among my students was immediately lost. In fact, all of them immediately wanted to sell! After Russia rolled their tanks into Ukraine and committed horrific war crimes, the majority of consumers and investors throughout the world found ways to fully sell all of their stock in Russian government-owned corporations.

Why is that? Do most people have a deep understanding that being a consumer or shareholder means having a certain moral responsibility? Or is it just an overreaction that is fueled by the media? To answer this question, it is important to understand the implications of stock ownership.

Moral Responsibilities of a Shareholder

As mentioned in chapter 13, *shares of stock* are certificates of ownership that an investor receives in exchange for investing money in a corporation. If you are a shareowner, you are a business owner. Once a corporation receives money from investors, the corporation buys *assets* (machines, land, property, etc.). These assets are then managed by staff who receive a salary so that they will, hopefully, be able to generate a profit while managing those assets. This profit belongs exclusively to the stock owners.

For example, if a small, start-up lemonade business received $250 from an investor, the business would hire a manager to buy a lemon-squeezing machine and some lemons, which they hope will generate sales that are in excess of expenses (i.e., profit). Given that shareowners "own" the profits, this would mean that a shareowner is a *residual owner*, effectively making any stock owner a type of business owner.

Often, however, stock owners do not fully realize they actually own the business in which they bought shares. Perhaps this happens because a shareholder is one of thousands of other owners, so it seems like each individual ownership claim is too insignificant. But that is not true: Ownership is ownership, whether small or large. Shareholders also receive regular dividend payments, which are additional evidence they own the profits.

Entitlement to profits is the most important part of business ownership, but another clear sign that shareholders are actually owners is that they are asked to vote on important matters. Shareholders receive voting packets in the mail every quarter, and to vote is to be counted as an owner; or put another way, to cast your vote means you are exercising certain rights within that business because you are part owner.

With their votes, shareholders are able to influence who manages the corporation. In turn, the managers must look to their shareholders before they make important business decisions. If shareholders remain silent, the business managers will assume the shareholders are in agreement with their actions, even if their actions are immoral. Financial commentator and researcher Martin Sandbu draws this conclusion: "Inasmuch as the corporation acts on the investor's behalf, the investor is a co-author of the wrongful act, and therefore morally co-responsible for it."[110]

Built into the fabric of a Limited Liability Corporation is an accountability system where management is meant to consistently look to their shareholders, whose interests they have been hired to represent. But as managers have looked to their investors, most Christians have been silent. This means that Christians who owned PetroChina stock while the corporation was funding a genocide bear some moral responsibility through an act of omission.

Quite often, the logic of being a "co-author of wrongful acts" is hard for my students to accept. But here is another way to look at this situation: Christian shareholders have an incredible opportunity to beautifully clothe our world with capital. When you gain a shareholder vote, you gain admission into the courts of cultural power and influence. As a shareholder, you have the power to change corporate policy, bring about greater creation care, or even replace the current CEO. You are united with Christ, who is all about redemption.

Timothy Keller, in his excellent book *Every Good Endeavor*, talks about how investors have the privilege of being gardeners of our culture:

> [Gardeners] do not leave the land as it is. They rearrange it in order to make it most fruitful, to draw the potentialities for growth and development out of the soil.... It is rearranging the raw material of God's creation in such a way that it helps the world in general, and people in particular, thrive and flourish.[111]

As you invest your money into the stock market, why not endeavor to use your elder-years reservoir to bring about cultural redemption? Why not proactively seek to cultivate a beautiful garden of tulips, roses, and fruit trees instead of passively letting others exploit and misdirect precious resources? Otherwise, overgrown weeds will choke out the beautiful plants that bring God glory. I encourage you not to allow the world to manage your money without the wisdom and truth that you possess in Christ.

Our Three-Part Response

How should we as Christians respond to the weighty responsibilities of owning shares of stock? One response would be to hide our money under a mattress, but as I shared in the previous chapter, this would guarantee a loss of God's money. I believe there is a better way—one that echoes the response of a man named John Woolman. He had strong convictions about the immorality of the slave trade, and he was initially ridiculed by his fellow

Quakers for his tender conscience. During most of his life in the mid-1700s, the Quaker church refused to condemn the practice of owning slaves. It was not until John Woolman began meeting and pleading with them, in earnest prayer and with patience, that hearts began to change.[112]

Like John Woolman, we should all strive to be sensitive about how our investments are impacting culture. And like Woolman, our first and best response must be to collectively seek the Lord, and then present a unified front through *shareholder activism.* This term refers to the efforts of shareholders to come together and voice an opinion about how the corporations they partially own should run the business.

This is all well and good, but realistically, who has the time for such endeavors? And if a group of shareholders is small, it may feel like a waste of time as well! Thankfully, however, the ability to consolidate like-minded voices has improved over the years. There is currently

When you gain a shareholder vote, you gain admission into the courts of cultural power and influence.

a vibrant marketplace of Christian investment products that seek to use their shareholder voting rights as tools to make the Christian voice heard (see wholeheartfinances.com/appendix [chapter 14] for more information). These financial firms are producing products that are competitive within the overall investment marketplace while also seeking to be redemptive. The best Christian investment products will actively be (1) endorsing, (2) engaging, and (3) excluding as part of their investment process.

Part 1: Endorse

If a corporation's products and services are clearly demonstrating love and engaging in service for others, a Christian investment product can *overweight* this corporation through buying a larger percentage of its stock, and fewer shares of other businesses that are not demonstrating clear redemptive power. This is also called *positive screening.*

For example, Brown's Super Stores in Philadelphia, Pennsylvania, sells suburban quality food in poor "food desert" neighborhoods, and Mexico-based Vinte Viviendas is working to ensure that low- and middle-income families have access to affordable housing. These are great businesses

Christians can endorse with higher than normal allocations in order to help influence culture in a redemptive way.

Part 2: Engage

Christian shareholders can attempt one-on-one correspondence with managers of the corporations they own, but it is much more powerful when a portfolio manager, backed by millions of dollars of pooled investor money, engages a CEO. As Christian investment products gather more Christian dollars, they are able to collectively have a more influential voice.

For example, in 2015, Hilton announced they would no longer offer pornographic films in their hotels in response to pressure from Christian investors.[113] Additionally, in 1997 a Christian shareholder of General Mills, Chip Kleinbrook, discovered that corporate money had been directed to Planned Parenthood, a provider of abortion procedures. Instead of simply selling his General Mills stock, Kleinbrook submitted a shareholder resolution to change their policy. His proposal received enough support to put pressure on management, and the donations to Planned Parenthood came to a halt.[114]

Part 3: Exclude

The most traditional way for a Christian investment product to respond to a corporation that is influencing culture in a negative way is to simply sell it from their holdings. This is also called *negative screening* or *divestment*. The business models of corporations like Playboy and MGM Resorts will never allow for successful Christian-shareholder engagement, so they simply need to be divested.

Often it is simply the threat of divestment that creates successful shareholder engagement, but divestment itself may also lead to positive change. For example, from 2004–2007, a Christian charitable trust engaged with a British publishing corporation regarding international weapons exhibitions that were organized by one of its divisions.[115] After three years of engagement and a subsequent divestment of their shares (less than 1% ownership), the firm announced the sale of its arms-exhibition division. The charitable trust then repurchased shares.

COMMUNITY-DEVELOPMENT FUNDS

While *redemptive investing* has been the main topic of this chapter, *redemptive banking* is another exciting development that you should consider as well. *Community-development funds* are investment funds that act like online savings accounts, but instead of using your savings to fund mortgages and car loans to relatively affluent people around the world, this redemptive banking opportunity lends to local small businesses who want to transform their community. Normally these businesses do not have access to traditional bank loans. See the exercises at the end of this chapter for more information.

WHOLE HEART EXERCISES

WHERE ARE YOU NOW?

As an investor, I tend toward behavior that is ...

❏ Apathetic. [Mark any statements that apply.]

» I would rather not change anything I am doing.

» I am potentially funding products or services that harm people, but I don't know for certain and would rather not think about it.

» What I invest in does not matter as long as I make money.

❏ Redemptive. [Mark any statements that apply.]

» I want to take full advantage of the power I have as a shareholder to invest in redemptive products or services.

» I want to have integrity in every aspect of my life, including how my savings may be influencing culture.

» I take seriously my shareholder responsibility to make my interests known.

How redemptive is your mindset when you invest?

NEVER CONSIDERED IT									ACTIVELY SEEKING
1	2	3	4	5	6	7	8	9	10

EXPLORE REDEMPTIVE INVESTMENTS

See wholeheartfinances.com/appendix (chapter 14) to access useful instructions and website links when completing these exercises.

Current and Potential Investments ·

❏ Evaluate how a specific stock or mutual fund is impacting culture by running it through a Christian "screener," which helps you to discern whether a corporation or fund aligns with or violates biblical values.

Faith-Driven Investor Marketplace

❏ Explore several Christian investment products that are currently available. Ideally, they are actively endorsing good businesses, engaging controversial ones, and excluding those that are unresponsive to active engagement.

1. Mutual Funds

2. ETFs

One way to lower investment fees is to choose ETF versions of any Christian mutual fund product. ETF shares tend to have the lowest expense ratios.

3. Private Equity and Seed Investing

Become a part of faith-driven investor communities to find redemptive business ideas.

In the end, the investment product you choose should align with your values, convictions, goals, risk tolerance, and financial situation.

Community-Development Funds

❏ Explore community-development funds.

» I have personally placed a portion of my cash savings in a community-development fund. This type of fund is not FDIC insured, so a risk of loss does exist, although this has not happened yet. In the few years I have been using these funds, I have earned a higher rate of return than what my online bank has provided.

» One other limitation is that you will likely not be able to access your money as quickly as you can access funds from an online bank, but it depends on the product. Regardless, it is wonderful knowing that your savings are helping inner-city families launch businesses that serve underserved communities.

CHAPTER 15

DREAM BIG— CREATE A SEA OF GALILEE FINANCIAL PLAN

If you aim at nothing, you will hit it every time.

ZIG ZIGLAR

Chapter 1 introduced the practice of *imprinting*, where we imprint our income to our new self in Christ. This has been a powerful exercise in my own life since it allows me to act with a whole heart as I decide what to do each time I receive money.

I don't always remember to do this, however. I remember one day when I finished my taxes and saw that I was due a large refund. I went for a run and thought about how thrilled I was that the refund was greater than I expected. As I began picking up speed, I imagined spending more and more of the refund on all sorts of home improvement projects.

After a few miles of daydreaming, I recognized I hadn't yet imprinted the refund to the Father. My first thought was to argue that a tax refund does not have to be imprinted. A finance professor can use lots of fancy financial language to make a case that refunds are not earned income and therefore should not be called "firstfruits" that one can give from.

But I felt no peace. While I didn't feel condemned, I wasn't comfortable either. I felt a tender nudge, like when a parent tries to gently wake their child from a nap. It wasn't until mile six that I finally stopped arguing and put up a white flag. "Fine, Jesus. Let me step back and declare myself dead to sin and alive in Christ." It was in that moment that a huge weight was lifted from my shoulders, and my running pace quickened. I didn't quite realize how much of a burden I had been bearing until I brought my heart back to wholeness through this financial decision.

Dane Ortlund, in his fantastic book *Gentle and Lowly*, describes how Jesus seeks to helps us in a gentle way: "When Hebrews 5:2 says that Jesus can 'deal gently with the ignorant and the wayward,' the point is that Jesus deals gently and only gently with all sinners who come to him."[116]

The moment I discovered Jesus is not a strict, disciplinary person and understood the wonderful mystery of how his generosity gently works to transform me, my heart's desire changed. It went from "What is the *least amount I should give* so I can spend or save the most throughout my life?" to "What is the *least amount I should save* in order to give the most throughout my life?" Put another way, I now wanted to excel in the "gracious act of giving" (2 Corinthians 8:7 NLT).

What Is Your *Telos*?

Theologians have long known that God created us as *teleological* creatures, meaning we will always be oriented toward a *telos*. A *goal* can be as simple as waking up tomorrow morning at a specific time, whereas a *telos* is about why you are waking up. What are you about? Adventure? Power? Comfort?

As Christians, broadly speaking, *our telos is Christ*. This is a type of "super" goal that orders and prioritizes all other "sub" goals.

James K. A. Smith, in his excellent book *You Are What You Love*, says, "To be human is to be *for* something, directed toward something, oriented toward something."[117]

This has been confirmed by psychologists as well. Researchers James Austin and Jeffrey Vancouver write, "Goals and related constructs are ubiquitous in psychological research and span the history of psychology."[118] One academic paper found that "the pursuit of personal goals can lead to a psychologically fulfilling life by providing meaning and structure to one's activities and identity."[119]

Since goals are a part of our fundamental design, the next most logical question to ask is, What goals, or telos, should we have? As Christians, broadly speaking, *our telos is Christ.* This is a type of "super" goal that orders and prioritizes all other "sub" goals. A financial goal is a type of "sub" goal that we should learn to prioritize through our ultimate goal of becoming like Christ and enjoying him forever.

Before we can prioritize, however, it is good for us to know what types of financial goals are available. While there are hundreds, I will take a moment to highlight those that are most common to our current American culture.

Level 1 Goals: Foundational

Level 1 goals are considered *foundational.* If they are not met first, unexpected emergencies will often lead to future debt.

- Establish an emergency fund: three to six months of cash savings
- Eliminate consumer and car debt
- Pay cash for your next car

Level 2 Goals: Building

Level 2 goals *build* on Level 1 accomplishments.

- Elder-years reservoir: Enough investment savings to sustain your generous lifestyle throughout your elder years
- Preschool, K–12, college, graduate school, certificates, trade

Level 3 Goals: Optional

Level 3 goals are *optional,* but relevant if Jesus is giving you the desire to achieve them as a pathway for his glory.

- Travel
- 20% down payment on a home
- Home improvements: renovations, additions, repairs
- Celebrations: weddings, graduations, anniversaries, milestone birthdays, special accomplishments

- Caregiving: disability, parents moving in, long-term care
- Second home: mountains, beach, near family, international
- Recreational vehicles: boat, motor home, camper
- Business start-up
- Leaving a bequest: Helping children buy their homes, helping grandkids afford college, supercharging ministry efforts

Two Paradigms of Financial Goal-Setting

Hopefully the idea of achieving some of these financial goals is exciting to you. When it comes to accomplishing a goal, there are two different paradigms, or patterns of thought. The first is when a person sets a goal and then measures their success based on whether the goal was achieved. This is called a *destination* focus. The second paradigm is to view goals as a *compass*.

1. Goals as a Destination

If I had a goal of saving $5,000 for an emergency fund, a destination focus would not deem me successful if I have less than $5,000 in my account. Likewise, if I made a goal to earn a 4.0 GPA, I would be a failure if I earned a 3.8.

The destination paradigm of goal-setting has been shown to lead to lower psychological well-being,[120] because achieving most of these goals is not totally in our control to begin with. And though we lack agency, the irony is that we often feel ashamed when we do not achieve a destination goal.

On the flip side, people who are not achieving their goals may target others as "in the way" and try to manipulate them to get the desired results. For example, if your spouse keeps overspending on groceries each month and you have a precious goal to save 10% of your paycheck, you may begin to manipulate them with threats, harsh language, or a diet of rice and beans every day.

Another reason the destination paradigm is not psychologically fulfilling is the disorientation and emptiness a person feels after achieving all of their goals—which leads to the question, Now what? For example, when I was pursuing my PhD, it was very easy to get caught up in the idea that life would be a permanent utopia if I could get past comprehensive exams and successfully defend my dissertation. But just as many people warned me, practically nothing changed after I received my diploma. I was still the same person with the same emotions and struggles (although I do believe that Dr. Pepper tastes better after becoming a doctor).

2. Goals as a Compass

Life is a journey. But if we journey without a compass, we don't really know where we are going, and everything is more confusing. Whenever I'm hiking in a dense forest, it is so refreshing to have a compass and know the direction I am heading. A compass acts as an objective guide and lets me relax a little bit, giving structure to what I am doing. However, even with a compass, I still must do the actual hiking, bravely crossing rivers and vigilantly watching for bears.

With a compass paradigm, goals give us a direction, but our ultimate focus is not on the destination. Rather, it's our process as we go about reaching our goals that really matters. And given that day-to-day processes are something we can largely control, psychologists have found that process-oriented goal-setting leads to better psychological well-being.[121]

For example, making a goal to save $5,000 for an emergency fund may direct you toward saving, but your focus will be on the process of saving itself. Your thoughts will center on creating the most enjoyable and sustainable process possible as you seek to spend less than you earn on a daily basis. The more enjoyable you can make your daily looking and tracking habit (see chapter 4), the more likely it is that you will reach your destination of saving $5,000.

Because my daily tracking habit is interwoven with spending time with Jesus, I enjoy it immensely. It's a time when I get to be truly grateful for how he has provided my daily bread so clearly. Whenever I focus on a process-oriented action that I can control and easily achieve, like tracking my expenses for three minutes a day, I will likely also achieve my financial goals.

Using a process-oriented way of thinking, we would never think about starving ourselves or manipulating our loved ones to achieve our financial goals since we want our process to be edifying and sustainable. What good is it if you lose twenty pounds on a crash diet, only to gain them back? In the same way, what good is it to save for an emergency fund through brute force, only to backslide and eventually lose it after a spending splurge?

Your Ultimate Financial Priority

So how *do* you enjoy the process of making a financial plan for your life? Put another way, once you identify your financial goals, how do you focus on the *process* of achieving them instead of obsessing about achieving them, no matter the cost?

The answer is in discerning your ultimate financial priority (i.e., financial telos). This is a type of *super*ordinate goal that provides structure and meaning to all of your ground-level *sub*ordinate goals (e.g., pay off credit card debt).

Having an overarching superordinate goal while making subordinate goals has been shown to supercharge a person's ability to achieve goals and enjoy the process. A superordinate goal connects your behavior to your ideal identity, which provides a high level of motivation for achieving all your goals.

Studies have also shown that having a superordinate goal can heighten the importance of traditional goals and increase self-control and flexibility.[122] For example, if your goal is to build a chair, you can heighten your motivation by connecting with your desire to be a loving person who ensures that others are well cared for. The subordinate goal is to build the chair, and the superordinate goal is to love others well.

> **Having an overarching superordinate goal while making subordinate goals supercharges a person's ability to achieve goals and enjoy the process.**

Without identifying your superordinate goals, you will likely be less motivated to achieve your financial goals. Following are two of the most common superordinate goals that I have seen others most naturally adopt with fractured heart finances, and a third superordinate goal that is most aligned to practicing whole heart finances.

Superordinate Goal 1: Stay Safe

Under a *Stay Safe* priority, your goal is for money to make you feel safe and in control. The larger your bank account, the safer and more secure you feel. Because money does lift us out of the dangers of poverty, we often believe it can lift us out of all dangers. Are you scared of losing your health? Money can buy the best medical care. Are you scared of losing your lovely home? Money can ensure that you never have to give it up. Are you scared of being robbed or assaulted? Money can get you fences, walls, and personal security. Are you scared of being alone or infertile? Money can buy you friends, romantic dates, and even children.

> The accumulation of wealth
> ... is a "false resting place."
>
> Heather Brown Holleman,
> *Seated with Christ*

Superordinate Goal 2: Have Pleasure

Under a *Have Pleasure* priority, your goal is for money to make you feel good and help you enjoy life. Having money is like having access to a luxurious day spa. The larger your bank account, the more you can truly enjoy the best of life—good food and beautiful things. And if material items are not important to you but experiences are, money will help you seize the day on the shores of Hawaii or the peaks of the Swiss Alps.

Superordinate Goal 3: Excel in Giving

Under an *Excel in Giving* priority, your goal is to have enough money that you can generously share with others. In so doing, you get to imitate Jesus Christ. While you deeply care about having comfort and being safe, you understand that they are not ultimately acquired through large bank accounts. God himself is the only source of true safety (Psalm 46:1) and comfort (2 Corinthians 1:3). Because Christ has already given you everything that is truly important and permanent, the

> We, who have received from
> the river of God's delights,
> pass it on.
>
> Leanne Payne,
> *Listening Prayer*

larger your bank account, the more you will gather others around you to share your good fortune.

With an Excel in Giving priority, you will likely rejoice like King David did after he rallied the Israelites to give their treasures for the building of the temple, saying, "Who am I, and who are my people, that we should be able to give as generously as this? Everything comes from you, and we have given you only what comes from your hand" (1 Chronicles 29:14).

> Living out radically ordinary hospitality leaves us with plenty to share, because we intentionally live below our means.
>
> Rosaria Butterfield,
> *The Gospel Comes with a House Key*

If this is your priority, spending and saving are tools that will help you maximize your sustained giving level and exercise radical hospitality toward your neighbors and friends. Like the Sea of Galilee, you will seek to maintain as wide and healthy of a giving outlet as possible. You'll use the tools of financial planning to become a more generous, more sustainable giver. Having an emergency fund and an elder-years reservoir will help you avoid future debt and ensure that you give generously throughout all seasons of life.

Unfailing Promises

One morning when I was at the beach praying, the Lord impressed upon my heart to give more than I should, at least according to my financial plan. I fought for a while, employing great arguments about "responsibility" and "stewardship." But in the end, I released my plans to the Lord and ended up giving more than "I should." After I did this, a great whoosh of relief flooded my heart. It was truly a *whole heart finances* moment.

Whether I stick to them or not, I love the process of making financial plans alongside Jesus. I am united to him through his death and resurrection. You, too, can relax as you make your own financial plans, because the Bible promises that when you bring your whole heart to Jesus, God will shower you with his gracious generosity:

He who did not spare his own Son, but gave him up for us all—how will he not also, along with him, graciously give us all things?

ROMANS 8:32

Which of you fathers, if your son asks for a fish, will give him a snake instead? Or if he asks for an egg, will give him a scorpion? If you then, though you are evil, know how to give good gifts to your children, how much more will your Father in heaven give the Holy Spirit to those who ask him!

LUKE 11:11–13

Why do you worry about clothes? See how the flowers of the field grow. They do not labor or spin. Yet I tell you that not even Solomon in all his splendor was dressed like one of these. If that is how God clothes the grass of the field, which is here today and tomorrow is thrown into the fire, will he not much more clothe you—you of little faith? So do not worry, saying, "What shall we eat?" or "What shall we drink?" or "What shall we wear?" For the pagans run after all these things, and your heavenly Father knows that you need them. But seek first his kingdom and his righteousness, and all these things will be given to you as well.

MATTHEW 6:28–33

Take these promises to heart as you create your own financial plan for meeting Level 1 foundational goals, building toward Level 2 goals, and opting for Level 3 goals that bring you enjoyment as they glorify God. As you spend, track, save, give, and invest, remember that the concept of whole heart finances is a process, not a destination. Give yourself plenty of grace when you experience setbacks or make mistakes, knowing that "in all things God works for the good of those who love him" (Romans 8:28).

WHOLE HEART EXERCISES

PRACTICE CENTERING PRAYER

❏ Before making your financial plan, fully immerse yourself in the centering prayer from chapter 2.

1. **Jesus above me:** *I receive Jesus, the Holy Spirit, and all of God's sweet material provisions. I receive more than I could ever imagine.*

2. **Jesus below me:** *God's providential nature, through the giving of his Son and Spirit, has planted me into the deep soil of his kingdom. As his adopted child, I am truly rooted in the house of God and have been transformed to have the same giving heart as the Father.*

3. **Jesus around me:** *Jesus is on his throne, using his people in a grand plan to redeem all of creation. Through my adoption, I am connected to this kingdom and the citizens of this kingdom, my brothers and sisters in Christ.*

4. **Jesus in me:** *I am in Christ and excited to do his work with the help of the Holy Spirit. I am called into the world to be generous with what has been given to me by the Father: the Son, the Spirit, my money, my time, and my talents. I do this in response to God's love and out of a cheerful heart. I will use the tools that make up personal financial planning to bring about a greater, more sustained giving lifestyle.*

IDENTIFY YOUR FINANCIAL GOALS

By practicing a good spending plan, financial margin will surface, allowing you to create an overall financial plan that will provide for your vehicles, education, home-buying, and elder years.

The exercises below will help you identity your goals, providing a useful compass as you dream big about your Sea of Galilee financial plan. Remember to think about the process that would be necessary for these goals to be accomplished. For a great discussion about how to connect a process to a goal, I recommend the book *Atomic Habits*, by James Clear.

❑ Identify your Level 1, 2, and 3 financial goals.

Level 1 goals: _____

Level 2 goals: _____

Level 3 goals: _____

❑ Write down what kind of superordinate goal (priority or telos) you want to aim for as you create your financial plan.

My superordinate goal: _____

❑ Spend time with Jesus asking him to reveal how these financial goals will help you love him in a deeper way, knowing that he purposefully created you with certain gifts and passions and planted you in a specific community. Pray Psalm 139:23–24 as you seek the Lord about your financial goals:

> *Search me, God, and know my heart;*
> *test me and know my anxious thoughts.*
> *See if there is any offensive way in me,*
> *and lead me in the way everlasting.*

YOUR SEA OF GALILEE FINANCIAL PLAN

This exercise will help you assess your financial life using the Sea of Galilee framework, where we respond to the Father's generous gifts to us (Jesus; the Holy Spirit; our time, talents, and treasure) by excelling in our giving.

❏ To the best of your knowledge, record your net inflow (income) and then determine how much went to debt payments, giving, and saving. Next, simply designate whatever is left as your consumption amount.

LAST YEAR'S FINANCIAL SNAPSHOT

NET INFLOW (AFTER TAXES)	$_____	100%
DEBT	$_____	(_____)%
GIVING	$_____	(_____)%
SAVING	$_____	(_____)%
LIFESTYLE CONSUMPTION	$_____	(_____)%

❏ Considering the Christian financial planning model presented in chapter 2, ask the Holy Spirit to help you identify what percentages you would like to have in each category over the next 2, 10, and 30 years.

CATEGORY	IN 2 YEARS	IN 10 YEARS	IN 30 YEARS
NET INFLOW (AFTER TAXES)	100%	100%	100%
DEBT	(_____)%	(_____)%	(_____)%
GIVING	(_____)%	(_____)%	(_____)%
SAVING	(_____)%	(_____)%	(_____)%
LIFESTYLE CONSUMPTION	(_____)%	(_____)%	(_____)%

NEXT STEPS

☐ Identify steps that will help you fulfill your Sea of Galilee financial plan over the next 10–30 years. Some possibilities are listed below.

1. Imprint your new money to your new self in-Christ, for the Father's sake (ch. 1).

2. Pray the Centering Prayer to acknowledge and receive the Trinity's role in your financial life (ch. 2).

3. Determine a giving system (ch. 3).

4. Set up a tracking system (ch. 4).

5. Set money aside in virtual envelopes for lifestyle expenses (ch. 5).

6. Take steps toward car and home ownership (ch. 6).

7. Determine your money personality and get in touch with unhealthy tendencies (ch. 7).

8. Build a three-month emergency fund to avoid future debt (ch. 8).

9. Become credit visible and aim for The 800 Club (ch. 9).

10. Pay off all consumer debt (ch. 10).

11. Open an online savings account (ch. 11).

12. Begin to save an elder-years reservoir (ch. 12).

13. Open a tax-advantaged investment account and prayerfully seek the Lord about how much to contribute, the possibility of maximizing your employer 401(k) match (if applicable), and fully surrendering any savings to the Lord and his purposes (ch. 13).

14. Choose redemptive investment products (ch. 14).

   * _____

   * _____

15. Meet with a financial professional who has the knowledge, tools, and time to help you achieve the goals you have identified. See wholeheartfinances.com/appendix (ch. 15) for a comprehensive list of the types of financial professionals you can meet with.

Sea of Galilee Financial Model

CONCLUDING THOUGHTS

I finally know what distinguishes man from other beasts: financial worries.

JULES RENARD

Early one morning while I was tracking my expenses, a $120 car-maintenance expense stood out on my credit card statement. I categorized the expense as "CCC (Creeping Car Crud)" and delighted in the Lord's provision, praying, "Thank you, Lord, that I can afford to pay this bill, which makes it possible for me to drive my vehicle. How wonderful is your provision of transportation that allowed me to surf yesterday before work. The smell and taste of the salty spray still lingers with me."

And this launched me into Psalm 34:

> Taste and see that the LORD is good.
>   Oh, the joys of those who take refuge in him!
> Fear the LORD, you his godly people,
>   for those who fear him will have all they need.
> Even strong young lions sometimes go hungry,
>   *but those who trust in the LORD will lack no good thing.*
>
> PSALM 34:8–10 NLT

Verse 10 is a surprising and potentially alarming passage. "Lack no good thing"? I have worked on skid row and other impoverished areas and seen plenty of people with a vibrant faith who definitely lacked good things—warm clothing, food, health care, and yes, finances.

As I was struggling through this verse, the reference to lions stood out to me. Why discuss young lions? What I found in Alexander Maclaren's classic commentary was a beautiful description of the attitude we must adopt as we manage our finances:

> "The young lions do lack, and suffer hunger." They are taken as the type of violent effort and struggle, as well as of supreme strength, but for all their teeth and claws, and lithe spring, "they lack, and suffer hunger." The suggestion is, that the men whose lives are one long fight to appropriate to themselves more and more of outward good, are living a kind of life that is fitter for beasts than for men.... One of the greatest works of fiction of modern times ends, or all but ends, with a sentence something like this, "Ah! who of us has what he wanted, or having it, is satisfied?" "The young lions do lack, and suffer hunger"—and the struggle always fails—"but they that seek the Lord shall not want any good thing."[123]

Even the lion, the king of the beasts in all its strength, must sometimes suffer hunger and lack. If we decide to become kings of our own lives as we gain the power and strength that wealth can give us, we are also fated to suffer lack and hunger. Excluding Jesus and deciding that we must fight for our own survival, we become like the beasts, relying on our own strength and eventually succumbing to our own limitations.

As we experience the goodness of Jesus, let us respond by growing in our ability to use savings and spending plans to excel in giving to others.

But those who seek the Lord have no need to act like a beast. Beasts are alone in their struggles, relying on their claws and strength for survival. But we are not alone. We are not like a lion that is ultimately responsible for taking care of itself and the pride. To borrow from the Chronicles of Narnia, we have Aslan (Jesus), the ultimate lion of lions, to lead us and help us. We not only have him but are also in him!

And this union is both spiritual and material. Jesus is not a person who will disdain our need for finances and material things, immediately telling us to "sell everything." Instead, he is lowly and gentle and even has material preferences himself (like goat cheese!) (probably). We can trust that the inventor of finances has very good counsel, is full of grace, and is waiting for us to trust him.

If we go into the financial world alone, we are fracturing our hearts. Instead, we can enter with a *whole heart*, with Jesus at the center, never forgetting that true satisfaction is found only in "tasting and seeing that the Lord is good."

As we experience the goodness of Jesus, let us respond by growing in our ability to use savings and spending plans to excel in giving to others. Let us never surrender to the temptation to view ourselves as alone in our financial fate, roaming the land frantically with a scarcity mindset. May we fear the *Lord* more than *finances*, and marvel at how this posture puts us in a position where we "lack no good thing." As Augustine of Hippo expressed in *The City of God*,

> God himself, who is the Author of virtue, shall be our reward. As there is nothing greater or better than God himself, God has promised us himself.... God shall be the end of all our desires, who will be seen without end, loved without cloy, and praised without weariness. [124]

Because we care so much about our finances, they are a highway to our hearts. It is my prayer that you allow Jesus full access to your heart, bringing a fresh awakening as you enjoy and worship the Lord through financial stewardship. I also pray that you respond to God's incredible generosity with a strong *telos* to excel in the grace of giving, and in so doing, glorify Jesus.

ACKNOWLEDGMENTS

I'm grateful to Gary Lindblad and Dave Bourgeois with the Crowell School of Business for fully supporting my efforts to develop the content of this book through empowering me to build biblically integrated financial planning and financial counseling programs at Biola University.

Anisa Larramore, Lynnette Pennings, John Ribeiro, and Cristalle Kishi from the Rose Publishing team were a joy to work with. Many thanks for your encouragement and skill as you took on this writing project. Thanks to Wes Wasson for providing a lovely place for me to write during my writer's retreat.

Most importantly, I'm thankful to my wife, Tammy, who often served as wind in my writing sails with her great enthusiasm and support—and to my kids, Sage and Silas, who teach me so much about God's love that I must write about what I learn from them.

NOTES

Introduction

1   Sarah Newcomb, *Loaded: Money, Psychology, and How to Get Ahead without Leaving Your Values Behind* (Hoboken, New Jersey: Wiley, 2016), 36.

2   Adam Grant, *Give and Take* (New York: Penguin, 2013), 53.

3   Matthew 19:16–22; Mark 10:17–27; Luke 18:18–30.

PART 1—Bring Your Whole Heart: Invite Jesus into Your Financial Life

Chapter 1: The Most Dangerous Question

4   Key & Peele, "God Visits a Prayer Group." February 11, 2021, 1:26. *YouTube: https://youtu.be/asnQGz7BdfI.*

5   Thank you, Mike Eerie, for providing this sermon illustration.

6   Alexandria White, "73% of Americans Rank Their Finances as the No. 1 Stress in Life, according to New Capital One CreditWise Survey." Updated December 29, 2022. *CNBC Select: https://www.cnbc.com/select/73-percent-of-americans-rank-finances -as-the-number-one-stress-in-life/.*

7   Kathleen Raine, "Worry about Money," *The Pythoness and Other Poems* (London: Hamish Hamilton, 1949), 24.

8   Goop Editors, "Are You Struggling with Financial PTSD?" April 26, 2018. *Goop: https://goop.com/wellness/career-money/are-you-struggling-with-financial-ptsd/.*

9   Shane Enete, "Three Essays on the Relationship between Emotions and Financial Resources," abstract (PhD diss., Kansas State University, 2020). *Kansas State University: https://krex.k-state.edu/bitstream/handle/2097/40877/ShaneEnete2020 .pdf?sequence=3.*

10   Megan Leonhardt, "41% of Americans Would Be Able to Cover a $1,000 Emergency with Savings." January 22, 2020. *CNBC Make It: https://www.cnbc .com/2020/01/21/41-percent-of-americans-would-be-able-to-cover-1000-dollar -emergency-with-savings.html.*

11   Lane Gillespie, "Average American Debt Statistics." January 13, 2023. *Bankrate: https://www.bankrate.com/personal-finance/debt/average-american-debt/.*

12   Jing Jian Xiao and Kyoung Tae Kim, "The Able Worry More? Debt Delinquency, Financial Capability and Financial Stress," *Journal of Family and Economic Issues* 43, no. 1 (May 6, 2021): 138–52, *Springer Link: https://doi.org/10.1007/s10834-021 -09767-3*; Elizabeth C. Martin and Rachel E. Dwyer, "Financial Stress, Race, and Student Debt during the Great Recession," *Social Currents* 8, no. 5 (July 23, 2021): 424–45, *Sage Journals: https://doi.org/10.1177/23294965211026692.*

13   Audra R. Sherwood, "Differences in Financial Literacy across Generations," abstract (PhD diss., Walden University, 2020). *Walden University: https://scholarworks .waldenu.edu/dissertations/8984/.*

14 For a more thorough discussion, see Barry Schwartz, *The Paradox of Choice: Why More Is Less* (New York: Ecco, 2004).

15 Graeme Wood, "Secret Fears of the Super-Rich." April 2011. *The Atlantic: https:// www.theatlantic.com/magazine/archive/2011/04/secret-fears-of-the-super-rich/308419/.*

Chapter 2: The Wisdom of the Sea of Galilee

16 Fred Sanders, *The Deep Things of God: How the Trinity Changes Everything* (Wheaton, IL: Crossway, 2017), 106.

17 *Thayer's Greek Lexicon*, s.v. Strong's NT 3622: οἰκονομία. *Bible Hub: https://biblehub .com/greek/3622.htm* (May 1, 2023).

18 Howard L. Dayton, Jr., and Compass—Finances God's Way, *2,350 Verses on Money and Possessions: A Resource for Your Financial Discipleship Journey* (Orlando, FL: 2022), iii. *Compass: https://compass1.org/wp-content/uploads/2022/02/2350-Verses -Catalog.pdf.*

19 "Augustine of Hippo/On the Trinity." April 2, 2020. *Wikiversity: https://en.wikiversity .org/wiki/Augustine_of_Hippo/On_The_Trinity#:~:text=Augustine%20gave%20 classic%20expression%20to,compares%20the%20persons%20of%20the.*

20 Craig L. Blomberg, *Neither Poverty nor Riches: A Biblical Theology of Material Possessions*, New Studies in Biblical Theology 7 (Downers Grove, IL: Apollos, 1999), 84.

21 "Daring to Be Generous." May 17, 2015. *Saddleback Church: https://saddleback.com /connect/Articles/MAP/2015/05/18/Message-Action-Plan-051715.*

22 John R. W. Stott, *The Cross of Christ* (Downers Grove, IL: IVP Books, 2006), 37.

23 John Barclay, "Because He Was Rich He Became Poor: Translation, Exegesis and Hermeneutics in the Reading of 2 Cor 8:9," in *Theologizing in the Corinthian Conflict: Studies in the Exegesis and Theology of 2 Corinthians,* Reimund Bieringer et al., eds. (Leuven, Belgium: Peeters, 2013), 331–44.

Chapter 3: Giving Elements, Streams, Systems, and Flows

24 "Tithes." *McClintock and Strong Biblical Cyclopedia: https://www.biblicalcyclopedia .com/T/tithes.html* (May 19, 2023).

25 Leanne Payne, *Listening Prayer: Learning to Hear God's Voice and Keep a Prayer Journal* (Grand Rapids, MI: Baker Books, 1994), 14.

PART 2—Spend with Your Whole Heart: Make a Budget That Actually Works

Chapter 4: Track Your Daily Bread

26 Darlene Deibler Rose, *Evidence Not Seen: A Woman's Miraculous Faith in the Jungles of World War II* (HarperSanFrancisco, 1988), 148–50.

27 Apple, "Apple Card / Chocolate / Apple." April 15, 2022, 0:38. *YouTube: https:// www.youtube.com/watch?v=XhA9wNUg5cg.*

28 Robert Frost, "Money," *Poetry: A Magazine of Verse* 48, no. 1 (April 1936), 4.

29   "Financial Capability in the United States," 5th ed. (July 2022), 4. *FINRA Investor Education Foundation: https://finrafoundation.org/sites/finrafoundation/files/NFCS -Report-Fifth-Edition-July-2022.pdf.*

30   Douglas McKelvey, "A Liturgy for the Paying of the Bills," *Every Moment Holy*, vol. 1 (Nashville: Rabbit Room Press, 2017), 193–94. Used with permission.

Chapter 5: Plan Your Run Rate with Jesus

31   Mo Willems, *Let's Go for a Drive!* (New York: Hyperion, 2012).

32   "Table 1101. Quintiles of income before taxes: Shares of annual aggregate expenditures and sources of income, Consumer Expenditure Surveys, 2021." *Bureau of Labor Statistics: https://www.bls.gov/cex/tables/calendar-year/aggregate-group-share/cu -income-quintiles-before-taxes-2021.pdf* (May 24, 2023).

33   Richard H. Thaler and L. J. Ganser, *Misbehaving: The Making of Behavioral Economics* (New York: W. W. Norton, 2015), ch. 2.

Chapter 6: The Blessing of Tires and Roofs

34   For example, the average monthly payment was $578 in 2022. Jenn Jones, "Average Car Payment and Auto Loan Statistics 2023." April 26, 2023. *Lending Tree: https:// www.lendingtree.com/auto/debt-statistics/.*

35   Susan Meyer, "Average Miles Driven per Year in the U.S." March 27, 2023. *The Zebra: https://www.thezebra.com/resources/driving/average-miles-driven-per-year/#how -demographics-affect-driving.*

36   I. Mitic, "Car Loan Statistics That Will Make You Want a Bicycle." March 7, 2022. *Fortunly: https://fortunly.com/statistics/car-loan-statistics/.*

37   Mitic, "Car Loan Statistics," *https://fortunly.com/statistics/car-loan-statistics/.*

38   Ben Eisen and Adrienne Roberts, "The Seven-Year Auto Loan: America's Middle Class Can't Afford Its Cars." October 1, 2019. *Wall Street Journal: https://www .wsj.com/articles/the-seven-year-auto-loan-americas-middle-class-cant-afford-their -cars-11569941215.*

39   Jack Caporal and Lyle Daly, "Average House Price by State." March 9, 2023. *The Ascent: https://www.fool.com/the-ascent/research/average-house-price-state/.*

40   "Los Angeles Housing Market." Updated January 2023. *Redfin: https://www.redfin .com/city/11203/CA/Los-Angeles/housing-market.*

41   US Department of Housing and Urban Development Office of Policy Development and Research, "Report to Congress on the Root Causes of the Foreclosure Crisis." January 2010. *HUD User: https://www.huduser.gov/portal/publications/foreclosure_09 .pdf.*

Chapter 7: Discover Your Money Personality

42   For a more thorough discussion, see Brad Klontz et al., *Facilitating Financial Health: Tools for Financial Planners, Coaches, and Therapists* (Erlanger, KY: National Underwriter Company, 2016).

43   Miriam Tatzel, "'Money Worlds' and Well-Being: An Integration of Money Dispositions, Materialism and Price-Related Behavior," *Journal of Economic Psychology* 23, no. 1 (February 2002): 103–26. *Science Direct: https://doi.org/10.1016 /S0167-4870(01)00069-1.*

44   Patricia Highsmith, *The Talented Mr. Ripley* (New York: W. W. Norton, 2008), 236.

45   Eileen F. Gallo, "Understanding Our Relationship with Money," *Journal of Financial Planning* 14, no. 5 (May 2001): 46–50. *issuu: https://issuu.com/simplewebservices/docs /understanding_our_relationship_with.*

Part 3—Guard Your Whole Heart: Relate Responsibly to Credit and Debt

Chapter 8: Credit Predators

46   A pseudonym has been used to protect privacy. "The Victims of Payday Lending." *Center for Responsible Lending: https://www.responsiblelending.org/issues/victims-payday* (June 1, 2023).

47   Will Daniel, "'Turbulence Ahead': Nearly 4 in 10 Americans Lack Enough Money to Cover a $400 Emergency Expense, Fed Survey Shows." May 23, 2023. *Fortune: https://fortune.com/2023/05/23/inflation-economy-consumer-finances-americans-cant -cover-emergency-expense-federal-reserve/.*

48   Hanneh Bareham, "Payday Loan Statistics." February 3, 2023. *Bankrate: https://www .bankrate.com/loans/personal-loans/payday-loan-statistics/.*

49   Matt Schulz, "2023 Credit Card Debt Statistics." Updated May 25, 2023. *Lending Tree: https://www.lendingtree.com/credit-cards/credit-card-debt-statistics/.*

50   LastWeekTonight, "Predatory Lending: Last Week Tonight with John Oliver." August 11, 2014, 16:31. *YouTube: https://www.youtube.com/watch?v=PDylgzybWAw&t=34s.*

51   The Pew Charitable Trusts, "Payday Lending in America: Who Borrows, Where They Borrow, and Why." *Center for Responsible Lending: https://www.responsiblelending.org /payday-lending/research-analysis/Pew_Payday_Lending_Exec_Summary.pdf* (June 6, 2023).

52   Bareham, "Payday Loan Statistics," *https://www.bankrate.com/loans/personal-loans /payday-loan-statistics/.*

53   Bareham, "Payday Loan Statistics," *https://www.bankrate.com/loans/personal-loans /payday-loan-statistics/.*

54   Joe Valenti and Claire Markham, "Predatory Lending: Faith Communities Mobilizing to Defend the Vulnerable." August 18, 2015. *Spotlight on Poverty & Opportunity: https://spotlightonpoverty.org/spotlight-exclusives/predatory-lending-faith -communities-mobilizing-to-defend-the-vulnerable/.*

55   Jayandra Soni and John Raymaker, "Focus Introduction: Toward Sharing Values across Cultures and Religions," *Journal of Religious Ethics* 39, no. 2 (May 19, 2011): 193–203. *Wiley Online Library: https://doi.org/10.1111/j.1467-9795.2011.00472.x.*

56   Carter Lindberg, "Luther on the Use of Money." *Christian History Institute: https:// christianhistoryinstitute.org/magazine/article/luther-on-the-use-of-money* (May 11, 2023).

57 A. J. Arberry, trans., *The Koran Interpreted* (New York: Touchstone, 1996), 69.

58 See "Islamic Financial Market Size & Share Analysis—Growth Trends & Forecasts (2023–2028), *Mordor Intelligence: https://www.mordorintelligence.com/industry-reports /global-islamic-finance-market* (June 6, 2023); see also Adam Hayes, "What Is Riba in Islam, and Why Is It Forbidden?" August 23, 2022, *Investopedia; https://www .investopedia.com/terms/r/riba.asp.*

59 Cory Stieg, "MIT Study: Paying with Credit Cards Activates Your Brain to Create 'Purchase Cravings' for More Spending." March 13, 2021. *CNBC Make It: https:// www.cnbc.com/2021/03/13/credit-cards-activate-brain-reward-network-create-cravings .html.*

60 For a more thorough discussion, see Barbara O'Neill, *Flipping a Switch: Your Guide to Happiness and Financial Security in Later Life* (Ocala, FL: Atlantic, 2020).

61 Schulz, "2023 Credit Card Debt Statistics," *https://www.lendingtree.com/credit-cards /credit-card-debt-statistics/.*

Chapter 9: The 800 Club

62 65% of consumers "appear to have transitioned out of credit invisibility by opening an account by themselves despite their lack of a credit history." The CFPB Office of Research, "CFPB Data Point: Becoming Credit Visible," June 2017, 33. *Consumer Protection Financial Bureau: https://files.consumerfinance.gov/f/documents /BecomingCreditVisible_Data_Point_Final.pdf.*

63 "Loan Savings Calculator." *myFICO: https://www.myfico.com/credit-education /calculators/loan-savings-calculator/* (May 12, 2023).

64 Julija A., "20 Worrying Identity Theft Statistics for 2023." December 16, 2022. *Fortunly: https://fortunly.com/statistics/identity-theft-statistics/#gref.*

65 Federal Bureau of Investigation, "Internet Crime Report 2022," 7. *Internet Crime Complaint Center: https://www.ic3.gov/Media/PDF/AnnualReport/2022_IC3Report .pdf.*

66 "Facts + Statistics: Identity Theft and Cybercrime." *Insurance Information Institute: https://www.iii.org/fact-statistic/facts-statistics-identity-theft-and-cybercrime* (June 6, 2023).

67 Julija A., "20 Worrying Identity Theft Statistics," *https://fortunly.com/statistics/identity -theft-statistics/#gref.*

68 Nikshep Myle, "14 Identity Theft Statistics That'll Make You Want ID Protection." October 5, 2022. *IT Pro: https://www.itpro.com/security/privacy/367947/14-identity -theft-statistics-thatll-make-you-want-id-protection#:~:text=As%20exciting%20as%20 it%20may,higher%20risk%20of%20identity%20theft.*

Chapter 10: A Pound of Debt

69 William Shakespeare, *The Merchant of Venice* (London: Penguin, 2005), 20.

70 "Juliet Chung: Brief History of Debt." September 20, 2008. *History News Network: https://historynewsnetwork.org/article/54714.*

71   Ashwin Vasan and Wei Zhang, "Americans Pay $120 Billion in Credit Card Interest and Fees Each Year." January 19, 2022. *Consumer Protection Financial Bureau: https://www.consumerfinance.gov/about-us/blog/americans-pay-120-billion-in-credit-card-interest-and-fees-each-year/.*

72   Goop Editors, "Are You Struggling with Financial PTSD?" Updated April 26, 2018. *Goop: https://goop.com/wellness/career-money/are-you-struggling-with-financial-ptsd/.*

73   Elizabeth Sweet et al., "The High Price of Debt: Household Financial Debt and Its Impact on Mental and Physical Health," *Social Science & Medicine* 91 (August 2013): 94–100. *Science Direct: https://doi.org/10.1016/j.socscimed.2013.05.009.*

74   Daniel A. Hojman, Miranda Álvaro, and Jaime Ruiz-Tagle, "Debt Trajectories and Mental Health," *Social Science & Medicine* 167 (October 2016): 54–62. *Science Direct: https://doi.org/10.1016/j.socscimed.2016.08.027.*

75   Michael T. Nietzel, "New Study: College Degree Carries Big Earnings Premium, but Other Factors Matter Too." October 11, 2021. *Forbes: https://www.forbes.com/sites/michaeltnietzel/2021/10/11/new-study-college-degree-carries-big-earnings-premium-but-other-factors-matter-too/.*

Part 4—Save with Your Whole Heart: Growing Your Giving through Saving and Investing

Chapter 11: Bank as Base Camp

76   As of 2023, the standard deposit insurance coverage limit is $250,000 per depositor, per FDIC-insured bank, per ownership category.

77   Shirin Ali, "One in 10 Homes in the US Affected by Climate Change Disasters in 2021, Report Says." February 23, 2022. *Changing America: https://thehill.com/changing-america/sustainability/infrastructure/595489-one-in-10-homes-in-the-us-affected-by-climate/.*

78   "Burglary Statistics." Updated January 31, 2023. *The Zebra: https://www.thezebra.com/resources/research/burglary-statistics/#statistics-2020.*

79   John C. Navarro and George E. Higgins, "Familial Identity Theft," *American Journal of Criminal Justice* 42 (March 2017): 218–30. *Springer Link: https://doi.org/10.1007/s12103-016-9357-3.*

80   An ACH transaction refers to an electronic bank-to-bank payment system that allows your bank to transfer money from your account to the vendor's account.

81   Megan Leonhardt, "Cutting Overdraft Fees Could Save Americans $17 Billion a Year—but Banks Are Slow to Make Changes." May 16, 2022. *Fortune: https://fortune.com/2022/05/16/cutting-overdraft-fees-could-save-americans-17-billion-a-year/.*

82   Sarah Foster, "Survey: Nearly Half of Americans Are Sacrificing Recession Preparedness by Paying Checking Fees." January 17, 2023. *Bankrate: https://www.bankrate.com/banking/checking-fees-survey/.*

83   Jane Austen, *Pride and Prejudice* (New York: Barnes & Noble Classics, 2003), 340.

84 "Pride & Prejudice (2005): Carey Mulligan: Kitty Bennet." *IMDB: https://www .imdb.com/title/tt0414387/characters/nm1659547* (June 9, 2023).

85 Elena Holodny, "The 5,000-Year History of Interest Rates Shows Just How Historically Low US Rates Are Right Now." June 17, 2016. *Insider: https://www .businessinsider.com/chart-5000-years-of-interest-rates-history-2016-6.*

86 Holodny, "The 5,000-Year History of Interest Rates," *https://www.businessinsider.com /chart-5000-years-of-interest-rates-history-2016-6.*

87 Dion Rabouin, "The $42 Billion Question: Why Aren't Americans Ditching Big Banks?" December 8, 2022. *Wall Street Journal: https://www.wsj.com/articles/the-42 -billion-question-why-arent-americans-ditching-big-banks-11670472623.*

Chapter 12: Gathering an Elder-Years Reservoir

88 Natasha Solo-Lyons, "Your Evening Briefing: One in Four Americans Have No Retirement Savings." April 17, 2023. *Bloomberg: https://www.bloomberg.com/news /newsletters/2023-04-17/bloomberg-evening-briefing-one-in-four-americans-have-no -retirement-savings.*

89 W. Andrew Achenbaum, *Old Age in the New Land: The American Experience Since 1790* (Baltimore: Johns Hopkins University Press, 1978), 22.

90 Merriam-Webster.com Dictionary, s.v. "retired." *https://www.merriam-webster.com /dictionary/retired* (June 8, 2023).

91 Esteban Calvo, "Does Working Longer Make People Healthier and Happier?" 2005. *Boston College: https://crr.bc.edu/wp-content/uploads/2006/02/wob_2.pdf.*

92 Nicole Torres, "You're Likely to Live Longer If You Retire After 65." October 2016. *Harvard Business Review: https://hbr.org/2016/10/youre-likely-to-live-longer-if-you -retire-after-65#:~:text=Working%20an%20extra%20year%20 decreases,%25%2C%20a%20new%20analysis%20shows.*

93 Timothy Keller, *Every Good Endeavor* (New York: Dutton, 2012), 21.

94 Ellen Rhoads Holmes and Lowell D. Holmes, *Other Cultures, Elder Years*, 2nd ed. (Thousand Oaks, CA: Sage, 1995), 74.

95 Dana George, "Why You Should Never Depend on Your Partner for Financial Support." July 17, 2021. *The Ascent: https://www.fool.com/the-ascent/banks/articles /why-you-should-never-depend-on-your-partner-for-financial-support/.*

96 Brittany King, "Those Who Married Once More Likely Than Others to Have Retirement Savings." January 13, 2022. *United Stated Census Bureau: https://www .census.gov/library/stories/2022/01/women-more-likely-than-men-to-have-no-retirement -savings.html.*

97 Jack VanDerhei, PhD, "The Impact of Adding an Automatically Enrolled Loan Protection Program to 401(k) Plans." EBRI, no. 551 (February 24, 2022): 3. *Employee Benefit Research Institute: https://www.ebri.org/docs/default-source/ebri-issue -brief/ebri_ib_551_kloans-24feb22.pdf?sfvrsn=e0f43b2f_2.*

98   Hal E. Hershfield, et al., "Increasing Saving Behavior through Age-Progressed Renderings of the Future Self," *Journal of Marketing Research* 48, SPL (February 2011): S23–S37. *Sage Journals: https://doi.org/10.1509/jmkr.48.SPL.S23.*

99   "Compound Interest Is Man's Greatest Invention." October 31, 2011. *Quote Investigator: https://quoteinvestigator.com/2011/10/31/compound-interest/.*

100   "Bill & Vonette Bright." *Generous Giving: https://generousgiving.org/bill-vonette-bright -surrendering-everything/* (June 16, 2023).

Chapter 13: Investing Your Reservoir

101   Chang Fu, "32 Must-Know Financial Literacy Statistic in 2021." February 15, 2021. *Possible Finance: https://www.possiblefinance.com/blog/financial-literacy-statistics/.*

102   Paraphrased from Saturday Night Live, "Host Will Ferrell Digs Up His SNL Buried Treasure." November 20, 2019, 1:22. *YouTube: https://www.youtube.com /watch?v=SB4ebtdBkkI.*

103   Ron Harris, "A New Understanding of the History of Limited Liability: An Invitation for Theoretical Reframing." August 29, 2019. *Harvard Law School Forum on Corporate Governance: https://corpgov.law.harvard.edu/2019/08/29/a-new -understanding-of-the-history-of-limited-liability-an-invitation-for-theoretical -reframing/.*

Chapter 14: The Redemptive Power of Your Reservoir

104   Merriam-Webster.com Dictionary, s.v. "invest." *https://www.merriam-webster.com /dictionary/invest* (June 19, 2023).

105   Rob West, "God as Investor with Jason Myhre." September 28, 2022. *Faith & Finance: https://bottradionetwork.com/ministry/faith-and-finance/2022-09-28-god-as -investor-with-jason-myhre/.*

106   Merriam-Webster.com Dictionary, s.v. "integrity." *https://www.merriam-webster.com /dictionary/integrity* (June 23, 2023).

107   Louise A. Mitchell, "Integrity and Virtue: The Forming of Good Character," *Linacre Quarterly* 82, no. 2 (May 2015): 149–69. *Sage Journals: https://doi.org/10.1179/2050 854915Y.0000000001.*

108   Giovanni Strampelli, "Are Passive Index Funds Active Owners? Corporate Governance Consequences of Passive Investing," *San Diego Law Review* 55, no. 4 (2018): 804. *Digital USD: https://digital.sandiego.edu/cgi/viewcontent .cgi?article=1166&context=sdlr.*

109   The Vanguard S&P 500 Index Fund, as estimated by *https://evalueator.com.*

110   Martin E. Sandbu, "Stakeholder Duties: On the Moral Responsibility of Corporate Investors," *Journal of Business Ethics* 109 (July 24, 2012): 97–107. *Springer Link: https://doi.org/10.1007/s10551-012-1382-7.*

111   Keller, *Every Good Endeavor,* 58–59.

112   "John Woolman." *Quakers in the World: https://www.quakersintheworld.org/quakers-in -action/62/John-Woolman* (June 27, 2023).

113 Michael Gryboski, "Hilton Removes Porn from Hotel Rooms after Hearing Sexual Exploitation Concerns," August 19, 2015. *Christian Post: https://www.christianpost .com/news/hilton-removes-porn-from-hotel-rooms-after-hearing-sexual-exploitation -concerns.html.*

114 Mary Naber, "Christ's Returns," *Christianity Today* 45, no. 11 (September 3, 2001): 86–87.

115 Usman Hayat, CFA, "Faith-Based Investing: Believers Engaging the Boardroom." February 13, 2013. *Enterprising Investor: https://blogs.cfainstitute.org/investor /2013/02/13/engaging-in-gods-name-believers-influencing-the-board-room/.*

Chapter 15: Dream Big—Create a Sea of Galilee Financial Plan

116 Dane Ortlund, *Gentle and Lowly: The Heart of Christ for Sinners and Sufferers* (Wheaton: Crossway, 2020), 54.

117 James K. A. Smith, *You Are What You Love* (Grand Rapids, MI: Brazos, 2016), 8.

118 James T. Austin and Jeffrey B. Vancouver, "Goal Constructs in Psychology: Structure, Process, and Content," *Psychological Bulletin* 120, no. 3 (1996): 338–75. *APA PsycNet: https://doi.org/10.1037/0033-2909.120.3.338.*

119 Jacob S. Gray et al., "Goal Conflict and Psychological Well-Being: A Meta-Analysis." *Journal of Research in Personality* 66 (February 2017): 27–37. *Science Direct: https:// doi.org/10.1016/j.jrp.2016.12.003.*

120 Edwin Locke and Gary P. Latham, "A Theory of Goal Setting and Task Management," *Academy of Management Review* 16, no. 2 (April 1, 1991): 480–83. *JSTOR: https://doi.org/10.2307/258875.*

121 Locke and Latham, "A Theory of Goal Setting," *https://doi.org/10.2307/258875.*

122 Bettina Höchli et al., "How Focusing on Superordinate Goals Motivates Broad, Long-Term Goal Pursuit: A Theoretical Perspective," *Frontiers in Psychology* 9 (October 2, 2018). *Frontiers: https://doi.org/10.3389/fpsyg.2018.01879.*

Concluding Thoughts

123 Alexander Maclaren, *Expositions of Holy Scripture: Psalms*, Psalm 34. Updated August 3, 2012. *Project Gutenberg: https://www.gutenberg.org/ebooks/7925.*

124 Augustine of Hippo, The City of God, quoted in Alister E. McGrath, *A Brief History of Heaven* (Malden, MA: Blackwell, 2003), 182–83.